FABRIC
SCULPTURE

THE STEP-BY-STEP GUIDE AND SHOWCASE

Dimensional Illustrators, Inc.
Southampton, Pennsylvania

Rockport Publishers, Inc.
Rockport, Massachusetts

Distributed by North Light Books • Cincinnati, Ohio

FABRIC

SCULPTURE

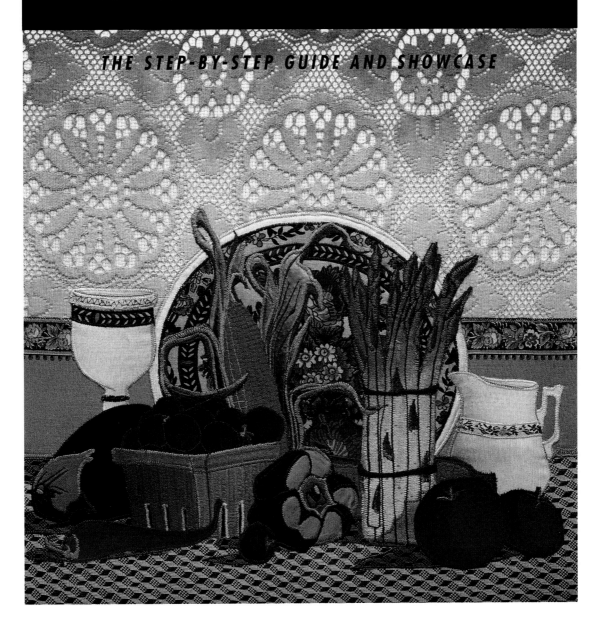

THE STEP-BY-STEP GUIDE AND SHOWCASE

Kathleen Ziegler
Nick Greco

Produced by **Dimensional Illustrators, Inc.**
Southampton, Pennsylvania USA

Published by **Rockport Publishers, Inc.**
146 Granite Street
Rockport, Massachusetts 01966 USA

Distributed to the book trade and art trade in the U.S. by:
North Light, an imprint of Writer's Digest Books
1507 Dana Avenue
Cincinnati, Ohio 45207
Telephone: 513.531.2222

Distributed to the book trade and art trade in Canada by:
McGraw-Hill Ryerson Ltd.
300 Water Street
Whitby, Ontario L1N 9B6
Telephone: 800.565.5758
Fax: 800.463.5885

Other distribution by:
Rockport Publishers, Inc.
146 Granite Street
Rockport, Massachusetts 01966 USA
Telephone: 508.546.9590
Fax: 508.546.7141
Easy Link: 62945477

Address direct mail sales to:
Nick Greco
Dimensional Illustrators, Inc.
362 Second Street Pike/Suite 112
Southampton, PA 18966 USA
Telephone: 215.953.1415
Fax: 215.953.1697

PRINTED IN SINGAPORE

Library of Congress-in-Publication Data
FABRIC SCULPTURE: THE STEP-BY-STEP-GUIDE AND SHOWCASE
Kathleen Ziegler, Nick Greco

ISBN # 1-56496-133-8

Creative Director & Editor
Kathleen Ziegler
Dimensional Illustrators, Inc.

Executive Editor
Nick Greco
Dimensional Illustrators, Inc.

Copy Editor
Tom McClintock

Designer
Jennifer Dunn

Typography
Deborah Davis

Photography
John Davis Step-By-Step Photographs Pages 34-36, 66-69, 82-89, 98-103, 114-119
Marianne Barcellona Pages 50-55
Will Mosgrove Step-By-Step Photographs Pages 20-23
Meghan Purvis Page 148
Tom Radcliffe Page 70
Bill Timmerman Page 34
Kathleen Ziegler Chapter Opening Photographs

Photos
Art Director Club, Inc. Page 10, 11

Hand Models
Barbara Maimon
Susan Tripp
Ann Ziegler

Artist's Rights
Paul Basista/Graphic Artists Guild

Cover Illustration
Margaret Cusack
Original Commission by Yankee Publishing Yankee Magazine's Recipe Calendar
From the Collection of Jack Miller

Cover Photography
Ron Breland

We wish to thank all the talented professionals for their assistance and support in producing Fabric Sculpture: The Step-By-Step Guide and Showcase. Thanks to the dedicated fabric sculptors from the United States and England for their hard work, patience and encouragement during the preparation of this book.

Special thanks to:

Deborah Davis

Jennifer Dunn

Tom McClintock

Thanks for all your valuable time and expertise,

Kathleen Ziegler/Nick Greco
Dimensional Illustrators, Inc.

CONTENTS

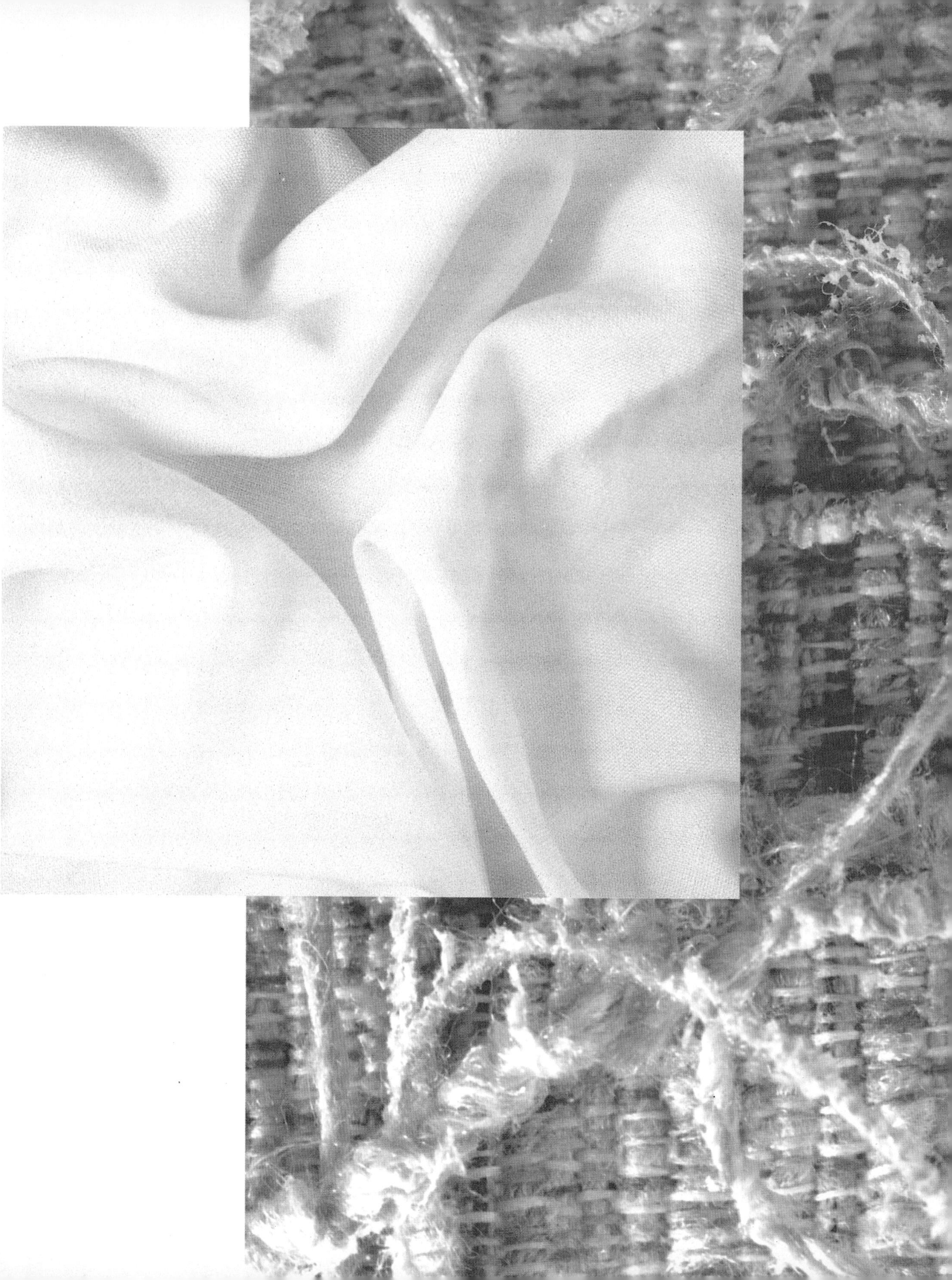

INTRODUCTION

Quilts, tapestries and needlepoint comprise most of our treasured fabric art acquisitions. Ancient fabric images date back to Egyptian times. A myriad of exquisite fabric artifacts chronicle the universal acceptance and popularity of this cherished and timeless art form. Time has always been a significant factor in fabric creation. The arduous labor required to complete a single quilt or needlepoint, has contributed to the complex changes in the fabric arts industry. Fabric artisans working together developed the commercial industry which today creates fine art fabric images. The contemporary industry that produces quilts, needlepoint, embroidery, applique and soft sculpture as art, has earned a singular place in the visual communication market. Today's innovative fabric illustrators produce dynamic 3-Dimensional images for the advertising and publishing industry.

The 1920's marked the beginning of 3-Dimensional illustration in the visual communications industry. Initially, advertisers photographed actual products to sell their merchandise. Later, elements of the products were assembled and then photographed to create a sculptural composition. The union of photography and sculpture, as an artistic medium, established the ingenious advertising genre known as 3-Dimensional illustration.

Textile companies were among the first to photograph their products for magazine advertisements. In 1929, an illustrator named Francis Feist was hired by the N.W. Ayer advertising agency to create an ad for the Sulloway Mills hosiery company. The product, woolen socks, was arranged in a simple composition and photographed for the ad. Sigrid Grafstrom is credited with being one of the first illustrators to use fabric in creating an overall illustration. In 1934, the McCutcheon textile company hired her to produce an illustration made entirely of fabric. She used a variety of textiles to create a picture frame. This illustration demonstrates the use of fabric as a creative medium for the visual communication market. In this photograph, the artist used fabric as the medium to create the illustration rather than to showcase the merchandise. This use of an actual fabric model in the advertisement marked the beginning of 3-Dimensional illustration in the visual communication industry.

The success of 3-Dimensional illustration can be attributed to the many talented and innovative creative directors and 3-D illustrators working in the 3-Dimensional industry worldwide. Advancements in the halftone photographic printing process have made it possible to use the camera to create powerful 3-D images. Today's talented 3-Dimensional illustrators continue to create exceptional ads, editorials, annual reports, brochures and calendars.

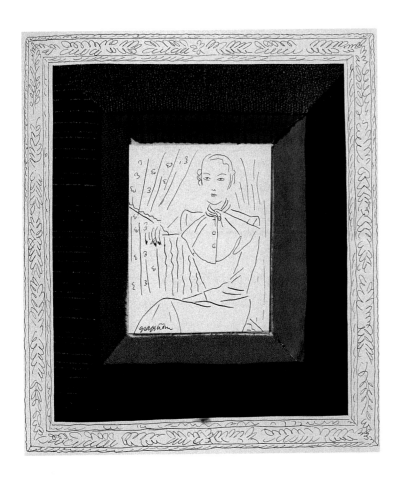

Each professional fabric sculptor in this book selected one project to demonstrate his or her approach, method and philosophy in creating fabric illustrations. Each step-by-step picture and caption provides insight into both the manual and creative processes required to produce each design. The 7 fabric artisans featured in this guidebook are all Gold, Silver and Bronze award winners of the 3-Dimensional Art Directors and Illustrators Awards Show. This international showcase of 3-D design was founded by Kathleen Ziegler and Nick Greco. Their goal is to promote an aesthetic appreciation of 3-Dimensional illustration in the advertising and publishing industry.

The 3-Dimensional Art Directors and Illustrators Awards Show recognizes the notable contribution of 3-D illustrators in the visual arts industry worldwide. These prominent artists represent the best fabric work from the United States and England. The book is divided into four chapters: Threadwork, Fabric Collage, Quilting and Soft Sculpture. The creative process and designs of each artist are presented in easy to follow step-by-step photographs. Every chapter concludes with exquisite full-color examples of each artist's portfolio.

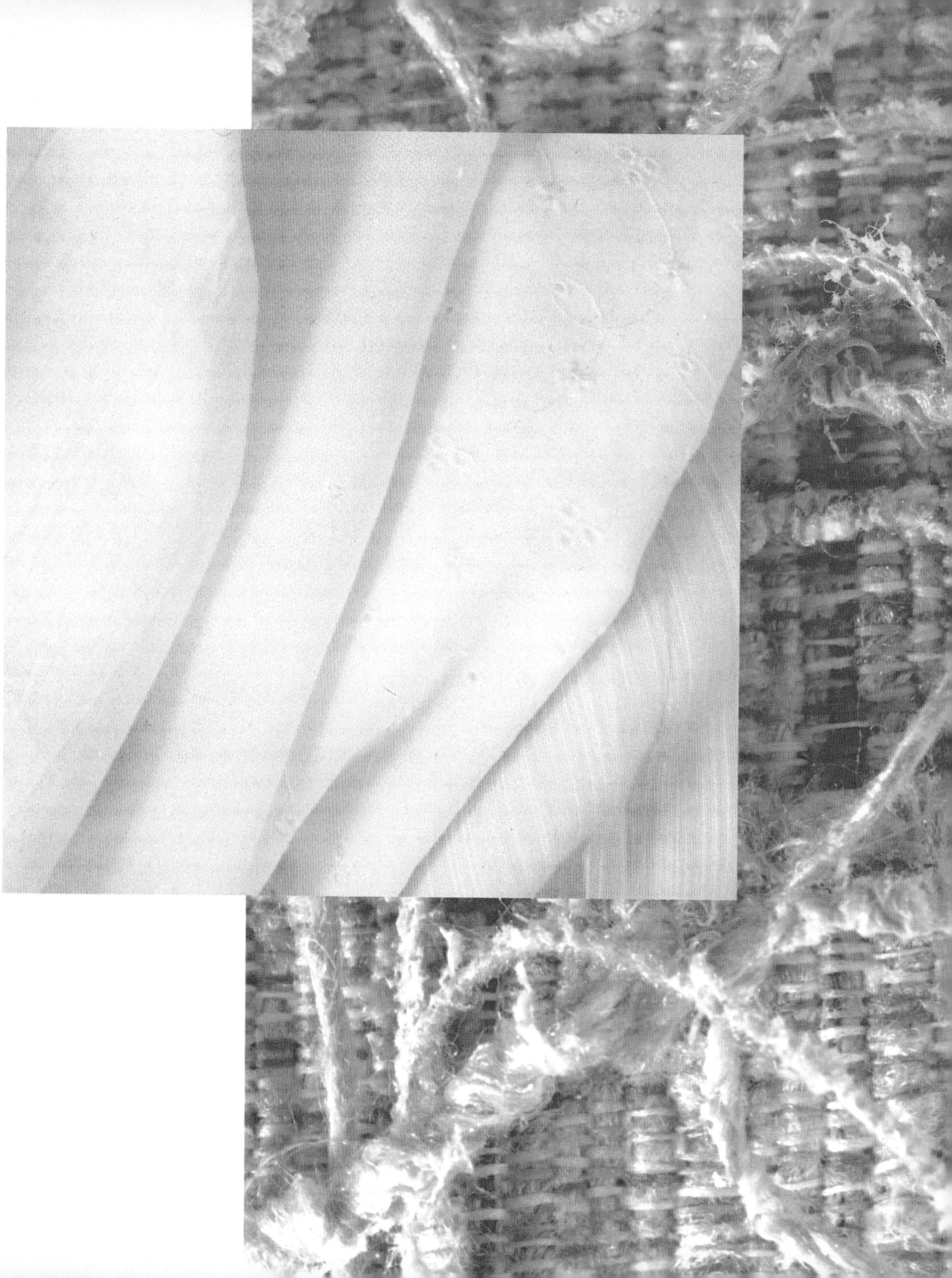

TECHNIQUES

Fabric provides the artist with a spectrum of textures, patterns and weaves for the creation of provocative 3-Dimensional sculptures. Since each type of material will respond differently when sewn, to achieve the optimum result, it is recommended that you test each technique on a variety of fabrics. The quality of your craftsmanship will depend on your ability to match the fabric to each stitching application.

Success as a fabric artist lies in a total understanding of the materials involved and their relationship to each other. The technical aspect of this methodical medium requires a repetition of sound methods and techniques. This is best achieved with consistent hand to eye control when working with the medium. Through practice, patience and proper usage of materials, you will achieve the excellence you desire. The following pages discuss the basic materials used to create fabric sculptures. By experimenting with a variety of fabrics, threads and techniques you can develop your own style of fabric imagery.

FABRICS

Fabrics are classified as natural or synthetic and vary according to weave, texture and weight. It is important to choose the appropriate weight to ensure that the fabric will hold the stitching or pinned application.

FLOSS

Floss thread is generally used for most threadwork techniques. The threads consist of six cotton strands twisted together. All six strands can be used together or separated and stitched as a single strand. There is an enormous range of colors available within a few different weights

BATTING

Batting is a cotton or polyester filler traditionally used in quilting. Batting demonstrates its versatility when it is applied to soft sculpture modeling.

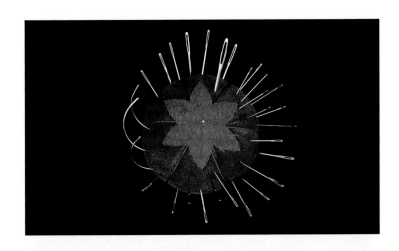

NEEDLES

Needles are divided according to eye-shape, length and point. Threadwork, fabric collage, quilting and soft sculpture each require specific needles. The wrong needle will put a strain on the thread and may leave ugly, unwanted holes in the fabric.

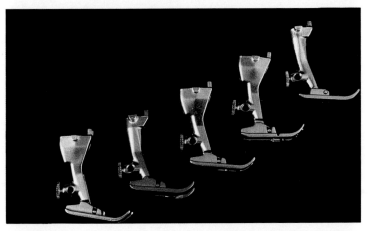

PRESSER FEET

These important sewing aids are paramount to the success of all machine made stitches. Fabric collage, applique and quilting stitches may require a specific presser foot for creating various stitches.

MACHINE THREADS

Sewing machines adapt quite easily to a variety of threads. Some are equipped with a thread tension adjustment which is designed to alleviate excessive strain on the thread to prevent breakage.

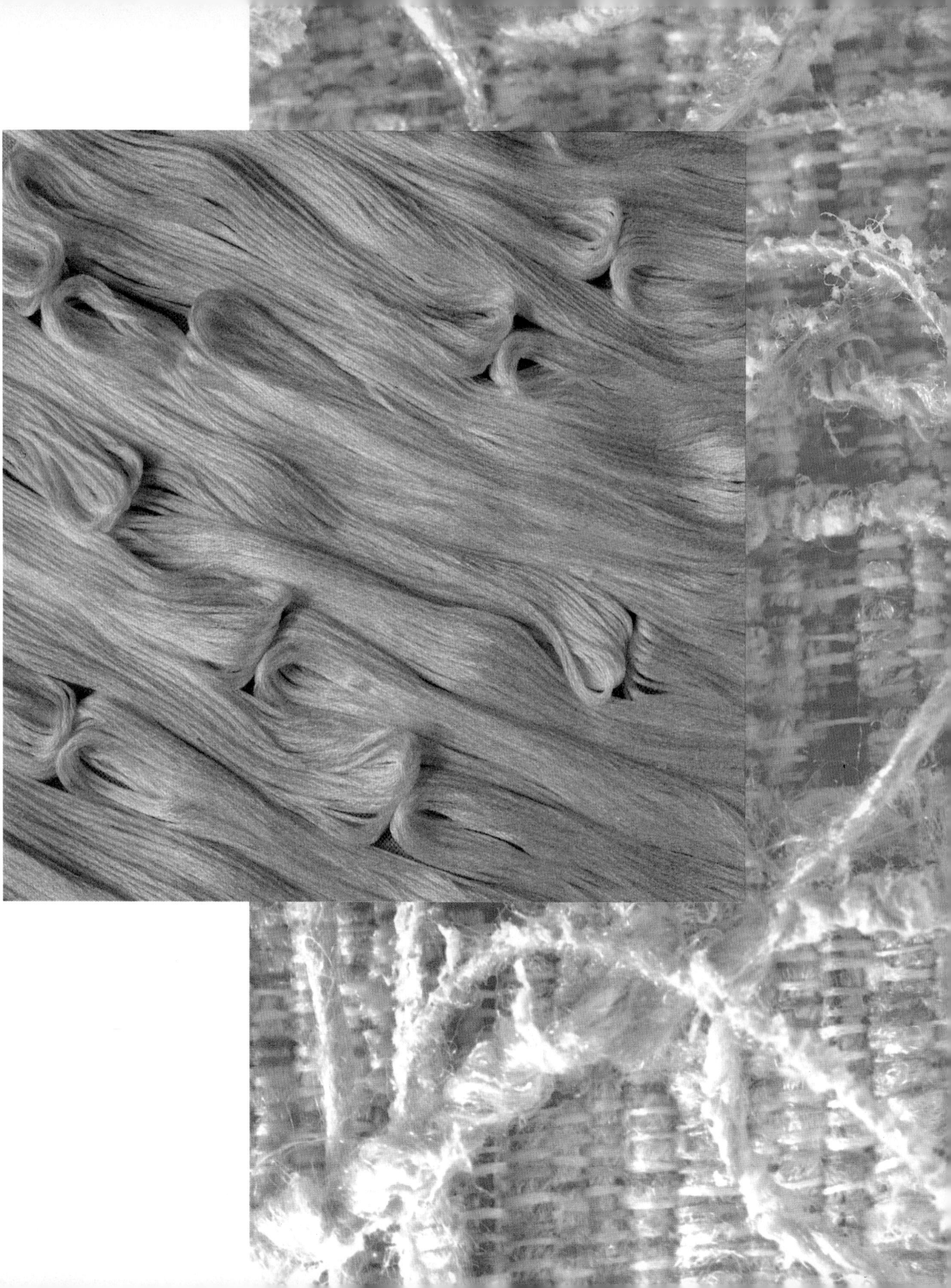

THREADWORK

A fabric illustrator uses thread rather like an artist applies paint. Embroidery, needlepoint and threadwork create flat areas of stitched thread that resemble brush strokes on canvas. The result is a warm textural surface that adds a very tactile element to the overall illustration. These diverse stitching patterns are as complex and provocative as any illustrative medium. Tonal areas of flat color result in graphic images, while subtle differences in the shades of the thread add style and impact to the composition.

The distinct styles of Anne Cook and Ann Morton utilize traditional threadwork stitchery with contemporary images. Cook draws her inspiration from images of Americana. Her use of bold rich colors enhance the needlework and add depth and warmth to the illustration. Morton's work is motivated by her lifelong admiration of folk art. Her forte lies in her unique ability to create a visually harmonious illustration combining paper and thread. Each artist demonstrates an extraordinary technical acumen which is reflected by their unique personal style.

Anne Cook

Drawing from folk images of the last two centuries, Anne Cook's threadwork style captures the essence of Americana. As a young child, Anne sewed, decorated her own clothing, and became intrigued with the tactile, sculptural qualities of embroidery. Educated in graphic design, she began, in 1985, to investigate fabric art as "a viable means of creating 3-Dimensional illustration." The familiar quality of her work features richly embellished detail, bold natural color and folk impressions reminiscent of times past.

Cook concentrates her creative talents on advertising, editorial and book publications. She prefers working in fabric because it affords her the opportunity to use a variety of textures. "I like the fact that fabric work has a real handmade quality to it." Anne believes that the warm tactile quality of fabric sculpture sets it apart from the sterile computer age of the '90s. Her attention to detail and to images of Americana add a very human touch to her work.

1

Anne's project uses an embellished embroidery threadwork technique. The idea for a fruit bowl was inspired by country style magazines, books on American folk art, and seed catalogs.

2

Several rough sketches are drawn on tracing paper. Once the final black and white sketch is made, she creates a color sketch by laying it over the final image and rendering it with colored pencils and markers.

3

The final drawing is enlarged to a workable size that will fit within a piece of muslin. Inexpensive muslin, which has more sizing in it, is used so that the paint will adhere without soaking through or bleeding.

ANNE COOK

4

The muslin is laid over the enlarged drawing and taped onto a light box. Colored pencils are used to draw the image on the fabric. The technical pen is used to detail fine areas.

5

The image is then painted with Dr. Martin's concentrated watercolors. These are not archival, they have brilliant color saturation but fade if exposed to light. Gradations are achieved by working wet on wet and applying the lightest color first. Care must be taken not to cross over the colored lines or the colors run together.

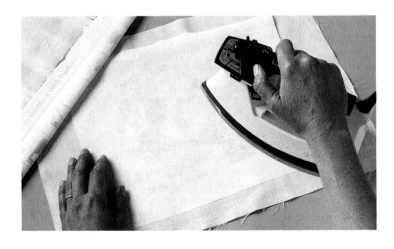

6

After the image is painted, Anne applies a fusible interfacing to the back. This makes the muslin opaque, prevents stitch show-through, and gives the fabric more body and stability.

7

Two threadwork technical reference books provided the appropriate stitches. The DMC thread book also inspired the embroidery floss colors. Anne chose the 6 strand DMC thread for its sheen and vibrant color.

8

Without the use of an embroidery hoop Anne hand stitches the "running" or "outline stitch" using 2 or 3 strands of thread. As she draws with the thread, she embellishes each element in the image. Fine detail is achieved by using only one thread. Other embroidery stitches are used where appropriate.

9

Once the embroidery is complete, it is pressed on a padded surface using a dry iron on the back to ensure that the stitching is not flattened. Steam or sprays should never be used as they cause the paint to bleed.

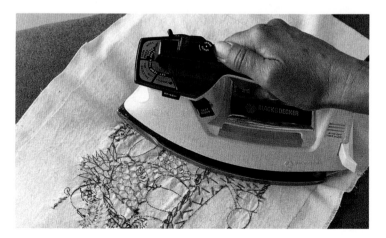

ANNE COOK

10

After trimming the muslin, archival spray adhesive is applied to the back and to a piece of double thick illustration board. The fingers are used to gently burnish the fabric tightly to the board.

11

Finishing touches, in colored pencil, further embellish the overall image. This surface rendering creates richer colors, deeper shadows and brings out the texture of the muslin.

12

Anne paints certain areas with Dr. Martin's bleed proof white paint. She uses this final step to highlight specific spots on the painted surface. The paint adds a bit of sparkle and dimension.

24

1
Bank Brochure Cover *First Chicago*
Threadwork
2
New England Cook Book
Yankee Publishing
Threadwork
3
Menu Cover
Wag's Family Restaurant
Threadwork

ANNE COOK

4

5

4
Calendar Cover *Yankee Publishing*
Threadwork
5
Winter Landscape *Finast Edwards*
Threadwork
6
Harmony Book Cover Logo
Putnam Berkley
Threadwork

6

7

8

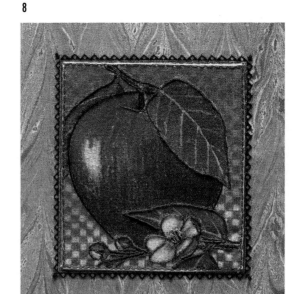

9

7
Herb & Spice Tin *Art Supply America*
Threadwork
8
Apple *C.R. Gibson*
Threadwork
9
Equity Sweet Equity *Wells Fargo Bank*
Threadwork

ANNE COOK

10

12

11

10
Main Street *Reader's Digest*
Threadwork
11
Harmony Book Cover *Putnam Berkley*
Threadwork
12
October Calendar *Paragraphics Printing Company*
Threadwork

13

14

15

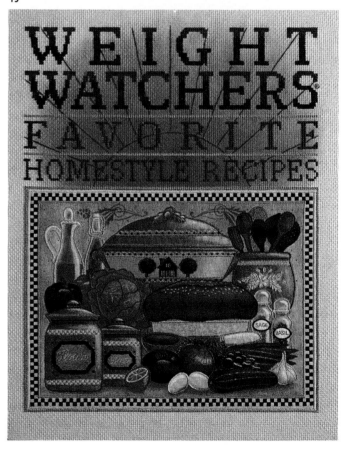

13
Baby Quilt Book Cover *Avon Books*
Quilting
14
Butterball Turkey *Beatrice Foods*
Threadwork
15
Weight Watchers Cover *Penguin USA*
Threadwork

ANNE COOK

16

17

18

16
Top O'the Morning *Self Promotion*
Threadwork
17
Baby Quilt *Becton Dickson*
Threadwork
18
USA Map *Met Life*
Quilting

19

20

19
Harmony Book Cover *Putnam Berkley*
Threadwork
20
Harmony Book Cover *Putnam Berkley*
Threadwork

ANNE COOK

21

22

21
Harmony Book Cover *Putnam Berkley*
Threadwork
22
Harmony Book Cover *Putnam Berkley*
Threadwork

23

24

25

23
Country Estate and Garden *Self Promotion*
Fabric Collage
24
Breakfast Still Life *Yankee Magazine*
Threadwork
25
Bread Loaf Landscape *Roman Meal*
Fabric Collage

ANNE COOK

26

27

28

26
Christmas Seeds Card *Self Promotion*
Threadwork
27
Bird and Letter *Modern Maturity Magazine*
Threadwork
28
Roses and Butterflies *Sunrider Vitamins*
Fabric Collage

Ann Morton

Ann Morton has woven a lifelong fascination with folk art into her professional work as an artist and graphic designer. As a child, she learned threadwork by sewing thread onto paper sewing cards, embroidering and sewing her own clothing. Although Ann primarily sews embroidery floss on handmade paper, she uses diverse materials that are suitable to the concept. Ann has worked as a fabric artist for six years. Materials such as newspaper, painted canvas, corn husks, office paper and old Levis have found their way into her creations. The result is an embellished contemporary image of colorful stitches and warm textural patterns. Ann skillfully fuses thread, paper and fabric into appealing visual illustrations.

Ann's ability to think in the third dimension enables her to create these images effortlessly. She feels she has "an affinity for folk art and images created by people...to express their life events." This fondness for folk art is evidenced by her use of traditional stitching details to embellish her more contemporary images. In turn, her creations communicate to the viewer a warm spirit of affection for her craft.

1

Before the physical creation of the artwork, Ann develops an image based on the concept. This illustration was designed to portray reactions to major life transitions. The visual representation is inspired by Spanish medieval art and Mexican masks with split faces.

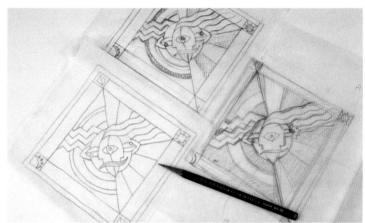

2

Rough sketches develop the general composition, and help direct the attitude and gesture of the concept. The visual idea is to look at the past and envision the future.

3

Ann overlays tracing paper on the final sketch to create quick color studies. These sketches help make the final design visually pleasing while conveying the idea.

ANN MORTON

4

Based on the final color drawing she selects appropriate matches of DMC 6 strand floss for the stitching. Later, she will be using only 3 threads for the stitching.

5

A variety of handmade papers are selected. They are stitched together in a contemporary fashion typical of traditional sewing cards. The colors chosen all relate to the concept.

6

Several copies are made of the final drawing. The elements are cut out through the copy and the handmade paper. Some of the shapes are cut a bit larger to allow overlapping and layering.

7

Once the shapes are cut out, the pieces are assembled. Each element is carefully glued together using as little adhesive as possible. Archival glue is strategically placed so as not to impede the stitching process. Several layers of glue can be difficult to pierce with a needle.

8

Certain shapes are transferred to the sheet metal using carbon transfer paper, then cut with shears. The frame is cut and handled carefully while gluing the elements to it.

9

Ann works intuitively, she rarely plans exactly how the stitching will be. She uses a variety of traditional embroidery stitches, including running stitch, french knot and cross stitch, to achieve color distribution and balance.

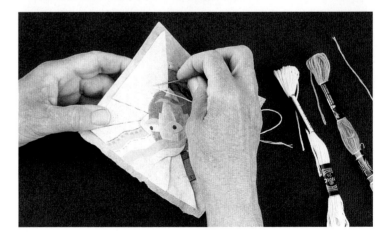

ANN MORTON

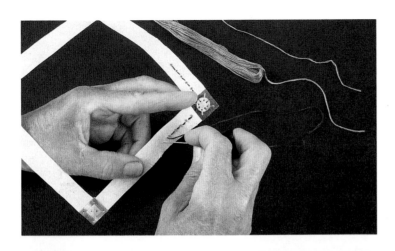

10

A running stitch is used along the outside of the frame. Each metal element is sewn into position with various stitches and colors. The floss, metal and paper become one cohesive element.

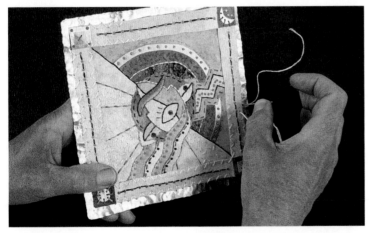

11

The frame is sewn to the square paper image. It is then sewn to an outer metal piece. Small holes are drilled to facilitate stitching. A leather thimble helps in sewing through the metal and paper layers. She stitches until she feels the balance of texture and color is right.

12

Ann uses the pillow while stitching because it allows her to push the needle through the piece and provide support for the delicate paper. The completed assembly is mounted on a larger piece of handmade Mexican bark paper. The background is embellished further until the overall image has the proper texture and interest.

1

2

3

1
Space Pear *Vim & Vigor Magazine*
Threadwork
2
Let's Talk *Phoenix Society of Communicating Arts*
Threadwork
3
The Perfect Copier *Office Systems Magazine Springhouse Corp*
Threadwork

ANN MORTON

4

© 1991 The Walt Disney Co.

4
Mickey Mouse in 30.375 Cubic Inches *The Walt Disney Co. The Art of Mickey Mouse*
Threadwork
5
Mickey Mouse (Detail) *The Walt Disney Co. The Art of Mickey Mouse*
Threadwork

5

© 1991 The Walt Disney Co.

6

7

8

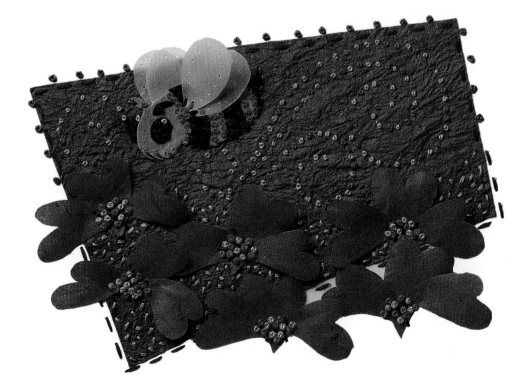

6
Barn Yard Species In The Desert *Personal Commission*
Threadwork
7
Box Full Tears *Personal Commission*
Threadwork
8
Bee With Heart & Flowers *Vim & Vigor Magazine*
Threadwork

ANN MORTON

9

11

10

9
Rabbit Through The Clouds Diary *Personal Commission*
Threadwork
10
Christmas Tamales *Scott Foresman Co.*
Threadwork
11
Theatrical Faces *Herberger Theater Center*
Threadwork

44

12

13

14

12
Art Snake *Arizona Portfolio*
Threadwork
13
Office Paper Pig *Office Systems Magazine*
Threadwork
14
Environmental Face *Self Promotion*
Threadwork

ANN MORTON

15

16

15
Keep Your Heart In The Right Place *Vim & Vigor Magazine*
Threadwork
16
Interesting Typographical Characters *Digitype*
Threadwork

17

18

17
Home Is Where The Heart Is *Del Webb Development Co.*
Threadwork
18
African Beehive *Self Promotion*
Threadwork

ANN MORTON

19

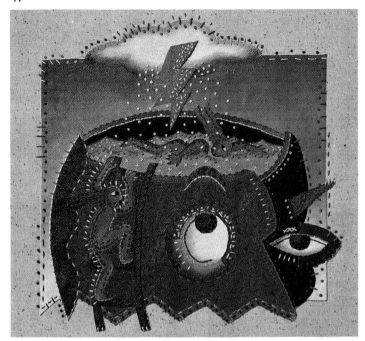

20

21

19
In His Head *Vim & Vigor Magazine*
Threadwork
20
Solitary *Vim & Vigor Magazine*
Threadwork
21
Cactus Paintbrush *Arizona Portfolio*
Soft Sculpture

22

24

23

22
Flower Power *Essex Entertainment*
Threadwork
23
Peace *Essex Entertainment*
Threadwork
24
Hearts 'til We're Old and Gray *McMurray Publishing*
Threadwork

ANN MORTON

25

26

25
Ms. Poindexter *Self Promotion*
Threadwork
26
Motor Mouth *Self Promotion*
Threadwork

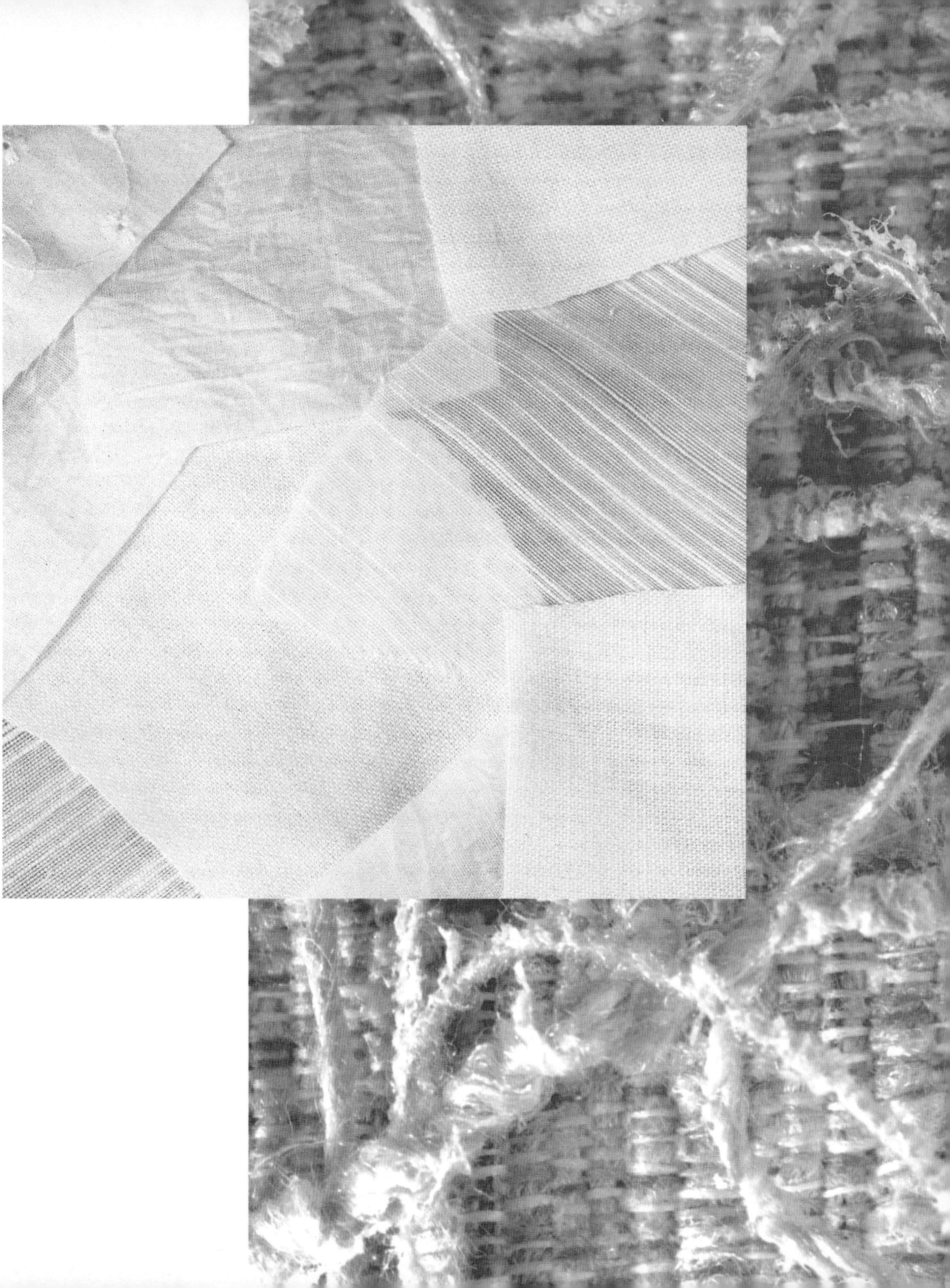

FABRIC COLLAGE

Appliqué is an ancient form of sewing interlocking fabric shapes onto a background cloth. This type of needlework was originally used to reinforce old, worn fabric. Today, fabric collage combines a variety of textures, colors and patterns into one configuration. The result is a melange of tones, shades and fibers that provides dimension to the overall illustration. Individual style is reflected by the artist's choice of materials, patterns and woven surfaces.

The works of Margaret Cusack and Jerry Pavey exemplify the variety of visual imagery made possible through this eloquent medium. Cusack's images depict emotions and expressions represented through the realistic rendering of figures and icons within the fabric. Her traditional fabric illustrations have contributed significantly to the awareness of fabric collage in the advertising and publishing industry. Pavey's approach is to use a variety of textures and bright rich colors. He assembles controlled graphic shapes to create his artwork. The effect is a collage of tonal surfaces with depth and tactile quality. While both artists have singular styles, their common thread is their use of Americana images.

Margaret Cusack

Margaret Cusack has produced a body of work directly related to her artistic exploration of texture and fabric since 1972. Working as an art director and designer after graduating from Pratt Institute, she decided to investigate and, indeed, create her own style of stitchery and fabric collage. She likes to "choose specific fabrics for texture, pattern, and color...to evoke nostalgic feelings." Cusack's sewing acumen has an astounding immediacy of color and texture that cannot be achieved with paint, pastels, or other media. Her singular talent has made her one of the most emulated and renowned fabric illustrators worldwide.

Margaret approaches each new project as a challenge. She specializes in Americana images as they seem a more natural choice for fabric collage. Although she does not limit her subject matter, she acknowledges it is most successful when there is a direct reason for choosing fabric over more traditional media. Whether evoking nostalgic Christmas scenes or traditional country settings, Margaret Cusack brings great originality, perspective, and skill to the field of fabric illustration.

1

Margaret was commissioned to create a country style music record jacket, cassette and CD cover entitled, "God Bless the U.S.A." Using her extensive collection of reference material, she creates a rough sketch of a house. The image is then elongated using her copier.

2

After generating several ideas for the style of the house, she designs the overall image characterizing the particular country style needed for the cover. She then creates a final layout that serves as a blueprint for the artwork.

3

The final design is drawn full scale as a pencil drawing on tracing paper. Only one finished sketch is presented to the client for approval. This is unusual because Margaret usually presents 4 to 10 sketches to art directors.

MARGARET CUSACK

4

Margaret assembles a palette of color from her enormous collection of fabrics. She and the art director agree on a bright Americana color scheme. The fabric prints are filled with brilliant primary colors; the checkerboard border, for example.

5

The fabric for the background sky needs to display a gradual blue gradation. This is accomplished by dying a piece of blue satin in a dark blue Rit dye and hot water.

6

Although many fabrics are chosen initially, only a specific few are actually used. Using fabrics scraps, she creates a small fabric sketch model of the image. This process allows her to experiment with various color combinations before the actual artwork is sewn.

7

The fabrics must be prepared before beginning any project. The selected material is heavily spray-starched and ironed. This process is repeated until the material has a paper-like stiffness.

8

She then positions the final drawing on a light box. Using a Stabilo pencil, she traces the individual elements onto the stiffened fabric. The Stabilo pencil draws a solid, even line on the textured fabric surface.

9

Once all the elements are traced on the specific fabrics, she carefully cuts out each piece with the utmost precision. This is essential because all the pieces will be sewn together like a jigsaw puzzle.

MARGARET CUSACK

10

The cut out pieces are placed on scrap cardboard and then sprayed on the back with 3-M Spray Mount. This professional adhesive is durable yet repositionable.

11

She positions them to a backing fabric called Poly-Pro Twill. This process prevents the fabric from slipping while being sewn together and ensures that the edges will be perfectly aligned.

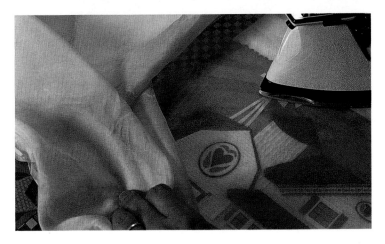

12

To further prepare the fabric art before sewing, the completed image with all the elements in position is ironed on the front surface with a pressing cloth. This process allows the adhesive of the Poly-Pro to set.

13

The logo for the title "God Bless the U.S.A." is created separately. Initial sketches are drawn to design the image. The lettering is then typeset on a curve. She later redraws the image and adjusts the kerning and a few letterforms.

14

The final lettering is then projected in her Artograph 1000J onto gold satin. She precisely paints in the letters with a 000 Winsor & Newton brush using Deka fabric paint.

15

The logo is then hand embroidered with aqua thread. Ironically, after all the work, the art directors decide not to use the stitched lettering for the cover title.

MARGARET CUSACK

16

Margaret uses a Bernina for all her machine stitching. Using the number 1 presser foot, she employs the zigzag stitch. This diverse stitch can be changed easily with the machine setting for particular designs.

17

The larger and outer elements are sewn on the background first. She then stitches the smaller elements in the foreground on top of the background to add to the dimensional effect. Final stitching is applied to the stars on the corner border.

18

The finished fabric illustration is stapled onto a wooden stretcher frame. This keeps the artwork square and straight for photography. The finished art is sent to the client to be photographed. Margaret retains the original piece and all rights.

1

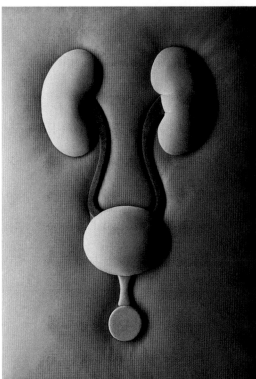

2

3

1
Catalogue Cover *Altman's*
Fabric Collage
2
George Washington *Self Promotion*
Fabric Collage
3
Kidneys *Emergency Medicine Magazine*
Soft Sculpture

MARGARET CUSACK

4

5

6

4
The New England Epicure *Bantam, Doubleday, Dell Publishing*
Threadwork
5
Peek Freans Shortcake *Peek Freans*
Fabric Collage
6
Hearts *Delta Airlines*
Fabric Collage

7

8

9

7
Uncle Ben's Canister *Uncle Ben's Rice*
Fabric Collage
8
Texaco Pincushion *Texaco*
Fabric Collage
9
Maxwell House Billboard *General Foods*
Threadwork
10
October Still Life *Avon*
Fabric Collage
11
Statue of Liberty *Avon*
Fabric Collage
12
Fulton Mall *Fulton Mall Improvement Association*
Fabric Collage

MARGARET CUSACK

10

11

12

13

14

15

13
Yankee Still Life *Yankee Publishing*
Fabric Collage
14
Great Waters of France *Perrier*
Fabric Collage
15
Heart *Emergency Medicine Magazine*
Soft Sculpture

MARGARET CUSACK

16

17

18

16
Katie *Avon*
Fabric Collage
17
Agribusiness *Touche Ross*
Soft Sculpture
18
United States of America Poster *American Express*
Fabric Collage

66

19

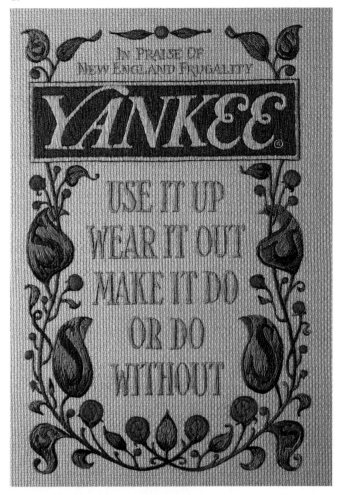

20

21

19
Jack & Jill *Seagram's*
Threadwork
20
Yankee/Use It Up *Yankee Publishing, Inc.*
Threadwork
21
Lamb *Celanes*
Soft Sculpture

MARGARET CUSACK

22

23

24

22
Holiday Lane *Macy's*
Fabric Collage
23
O Christmas Tree *Harcourt Brace Jovanovich*
Fabric Collage
24
Lungs *Geriatrics*
Soft Sculpture

25

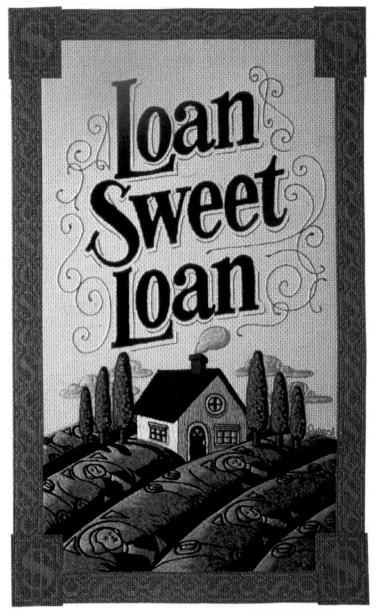

26

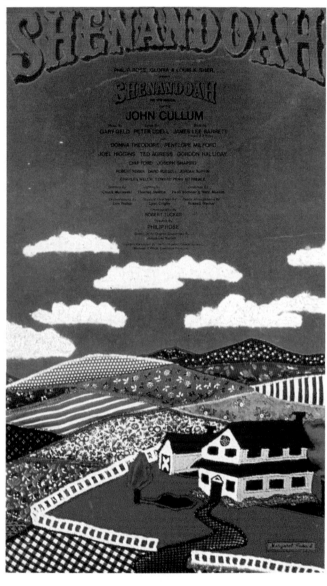

MARGARET CUSACK

27

28

29

25
Loan Sweet Loan *SONYMA*
Threadwork
26
Broadway Musical Poster *Shenandoah*
Fabric Collage
27
Baked Goods *Dolly Madison*
Fabric Collage
28
April Showers *Avon Calendar*
Fabric Collage
29
House and Family *Roxanol*
Fabric Collage

Jerry Pavey

Jerry Pavey uses rich, bright colors and heavily textured fabrics to achieve his signature style. As a professional art director he combined his sewing skills with his illustrative talents to create 3-Dimensional illustrations. Pavey's work often has brightly colored fabrics and prints which add depth and shadow to his illustrations. His technique of sewing pieces of fabric onto an overall background gives his work a look "reminiscent of friendlier times." This use of the intrinsic qualities of fabric, embellished with multi-directional sewing creates a most intriguing image when photographed.

Jerry feels his work is a welcome contrast to more "slick" photographic illustrative solutions. Pavey's images are often Americana in nature, but with distinct graphic characteristics. His work is used for editorial, advertising and book illustration, but recently he began producing limited edition prints. He embosses each print to simulate the detail and depth of the original. His work is technically sound, visually appealing and creatively innovative.

1

A rough sketch of the basic idea for the fabric collage is drawn in pencil. Then a color sketch representing the fabric color scheme is created. A third pencil version solidifies the image of the zebra while the added border enhances the Save the Animal theme.

2

Fabric selection for this piece is relatively easy because of the limited color range. He selects fabrics from his extensive stock of over 10,000 colors, patterns and textures. Bright colors are chosen for a contemporary look.

3

The image for the zebra is transferred to the front of the fabric. Using the pencil sketch as a template, Jerry draws the spaces for the zebra stripes on the white fabric. Then he draws the shape of the stripes on a black piece of fabric.

JERRY PAVEY

4

Once all the elements are drawn on the appropriate fabrics, he cuts each piece out individually using his Fiskar scissors. Since there are numerous zebra stripes, each one is handled in sequence.

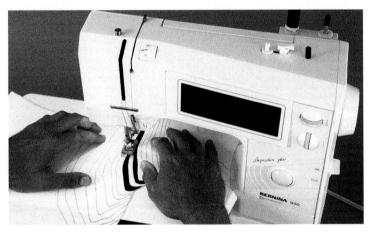

5

Wonder Under heavy duty fusing web is ironed to the back of the black stripes and glued into position on the white fabric zebra. Using his Bernina 1630 sewing machine, he sews the stripes using the presser foot number 1 in the zigzag mode. Adjustments are made to the horizontal and vertical controls for narrow satin stitching.

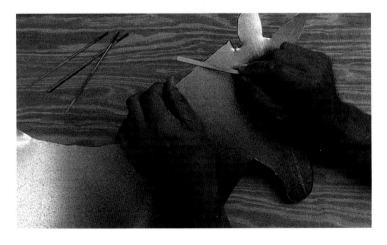

6

Jerry uses tin snips to cut pliable metal in the shape of the zebra. Since the silhouette will be sandwiched between two pieces of fabric, it is trimmed slightly smaller to allow for stitching the fabric edges together. All the edges are filed smooth to remove the razor sharp cut edge.

7

An outline lettering style is chosen for the border surrounding the zebra image. Using the Bernina 1630, the specific font size and spacing are programmed on the screen. The lettering is then stitched to the black border fabric.

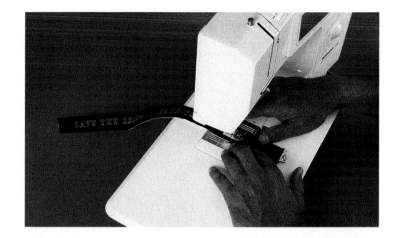

8

The background fabrics are fixed to a plywood backing board with spray adhesive. They are then stapled securely around the perimeter edge.

9

The finished metal insert is glued in between a backing fabric and the front zebra image. The edges of the front and back fabric are stitched together with a zigzag stitch. The fabric is then placed on the backing board and nailed into position.

10

The lettering strips are trimmed and glued to the backing board. Corners of the fabric strip are cut at 45 degree angles and glued down. Small black fabric squares are cut and placed on each intersecting corner. Metal stars are affixed with self-contained prongs.

11

Once the zebra is nailed into position, adjustments are made to give the image depth. The internal metal head and neck are gently pulled and bent forward to add depth and dimension when the model is photographed.

12

Just prior to photographing, the fabrics are sprayed with clear water. It is then placed under a heat lamp to dry. This process eliminates all wrinkles from the fabric.

1

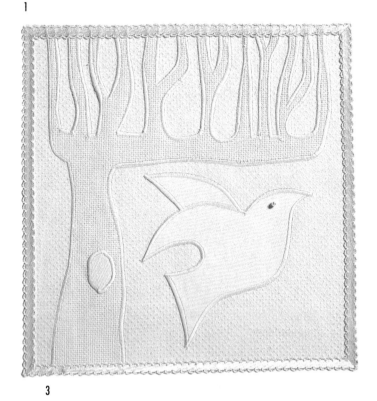

2

3

1
Tranquility *UNICEF*
Fabric Collage
2
What So Proudly We Hail *USIA Dialogue Magazine*
Fabric Collage
3
Christmas Goose *Self Promotion*
Fabric Collage
4
Pinot Noir *Wine Magazine*
Fabric Collage
5
Candy Store *S.D. Warren Paper and S&S Graphics*
Fabric Collage
6
Study In Apples *Self Promotion*
Fabric Collage

JERRY PAVEY

4

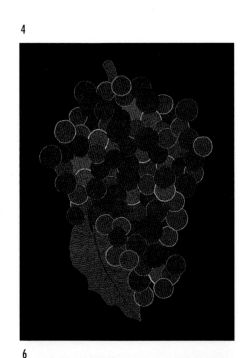

5

6

7

9

8

7
Metamorphosis *S.D. Warren Paper and S&S Graphics*
Fabric Collage
8
Sampan *The Brookings Review Magazine*
Fabric Collage
9
Philadelphia *Bell Atlantic/C&P Telephone*
Fabric Collage

JERRY PAVEY

10

11

12

10
America's Tradition *S.D. Warren Paper and S&S Graphics*
Fabric Collage
11
Political Constraints *USIA Dialogue Magazine*
Fabric Collage
12
Great Expectations *Alexandria Hospital*
Fabric Collage

13

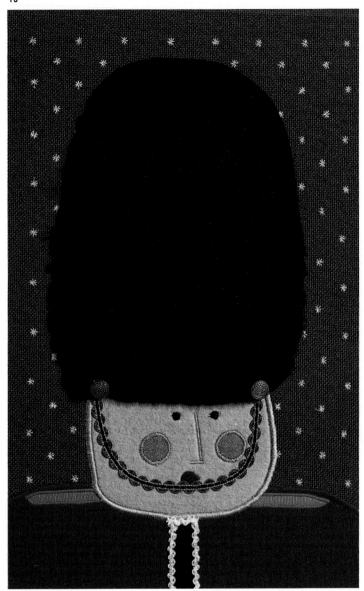

14

13
Sentry *UNICEF & Self Promotion*
Fabric Collage
14
The Sudan *Brookings Institute*
Fabric Collage

JERRY PAVEY

15

16

15
Martin Music *Martin Guitars*
Fabric Collage
16
Serenity *UNICEF*
Fabric Collage

17

18

JERRY PAVEY

19

20

17
Pledge of Allegiance *MacMillian/McGraw Hill*
Threadwork
18
Small Town *Investment Company Institute*
Fabric Collage
19
Christmas Greetings *Frank Gumpert Printing*
Fabric Collage
20
View From Capital Hill *S.D. Warren Paper and S&S Graphics*
Fabric Collage

84

21

22

23

JERRY PAVEY

24

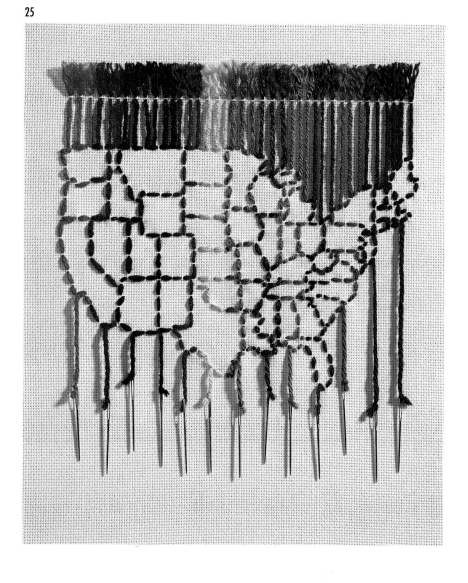

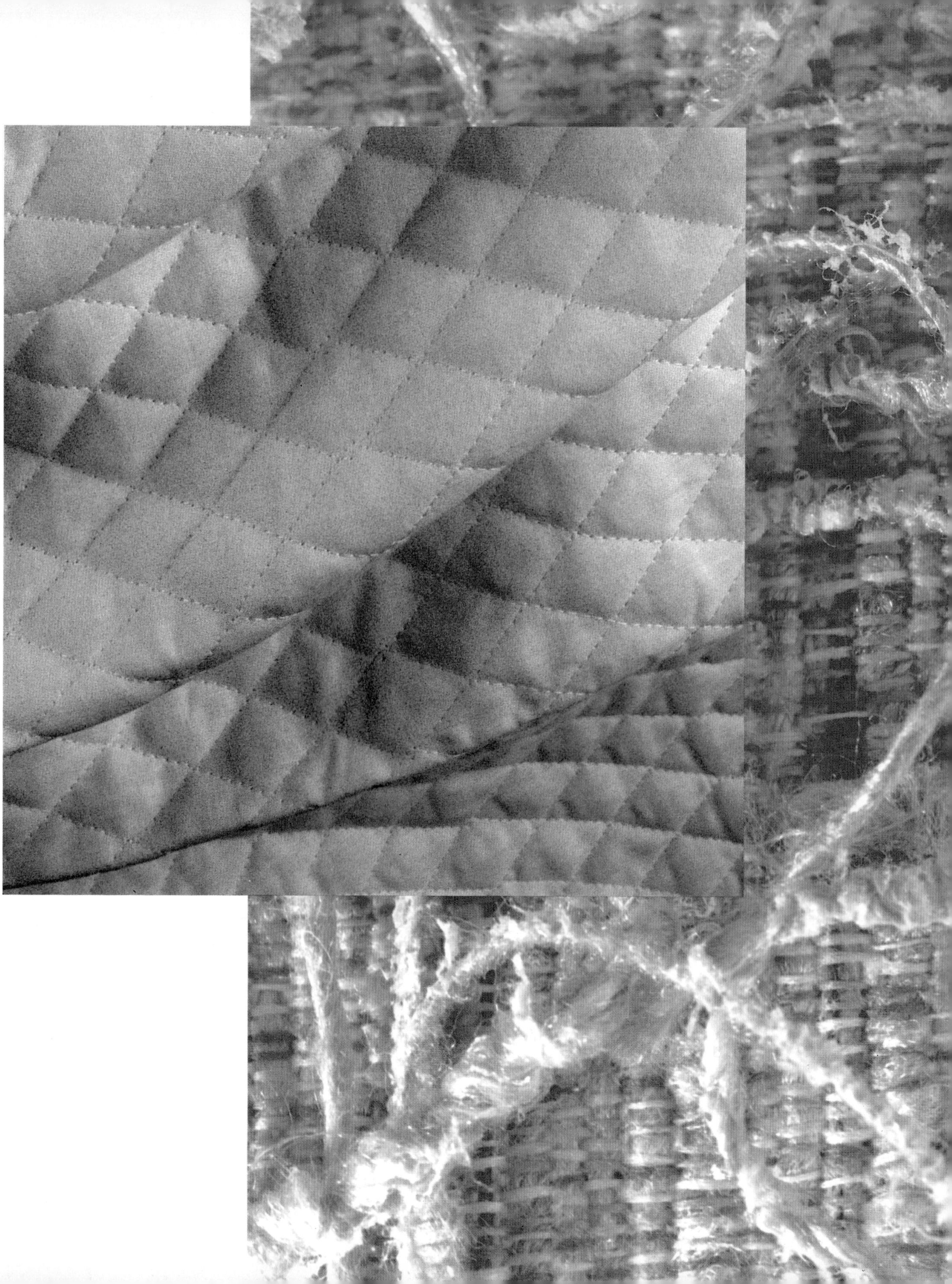

QUILTING

The art of quilting is one of the oldest craft techniques. There is evidence, in ancient Egypt, of quilted materials dating back more than 3000 years. Closer to home, quilting became an important handicraft for early North American settlers. Fabric remnants and scraps were transformed into quilts, and the modern art form began to evolve. Quilting can be considered a precursor to the popular recycling phenomena in vogue today. Bedcovers, friendship quilts and coverlets are the traditional items associated with this medium. However, quilting is also used to create fine art murals and 3-Dimensional illustrations for the editorial and advertising industry. The quilt's puffed surface relief adds dimension to the pictorial image, while its tonal variations offer the artist extraordinary conceptual possibilities.

Elaine Golak uses classical methods together with contemporary images to create quilted illustrations. She applies her unique style to the overall design pattern to produce an integrated effect. Her signature style features symbolic imagery combined with soft quilted texture. Golak demonstrates an extensive knowledge of color harmony and pattern relationships in a quilted, graphic approach that places her in a singular class of fabric creators.

Elaine Golak

Elaine Golak combines traditional quilting techniques with contemporary designs. She produces illustrations that have a warm and intimate quality rarely found in other mediums. Historically, wool or cotton is used in quilting. Elaine, however, works with everything from satin to muslin to achieve the right look. Golak places a premium on finding the perfect color fabric for a piece. She will occasionally use fabric markers to bring color or detail to small areas. The majority of Golak's work is display illustration, but individual commissions provide her with a creative challenge. For this fabric book Elaine creates a quilt based on an antique garden pattern.

Elaine believes fabric is an integral part of all of our lives - an extension of the most personal part of us. This universal feeling allows everyone to relate to fabric art on a basic human level. Having worked as a fabric artist for 15 years, she has developed a quilting style that features color, detail and distinctive stitchery. As an artist, she brings a contemporary viewpoint coupled with imagination, personality and flair to the traditional medium of quilting.

1

Elaine draws inspiration for her quilt from antique garden plot layouts. Topographical grid patterns created from the rows of plants are incorporated into a quilting design. Animal and vegetable images will be added as the design evolves.

2

From an extensive stock of material, fabrics are selected in keeping with the natural character of the garden design. Cotton prints are chosen which reflect the colors of a freshly planted garden and the organic patterns of vegetation.

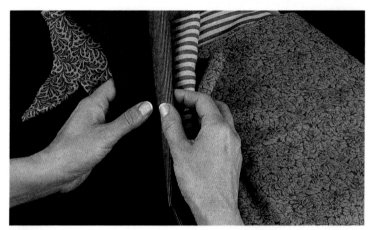

3

The chosen fabrics are marked in 1 1/4 inch wide strips with a fabric pencil. Elaine then uses her treasured Gingher scissors to cut out even parallel strips. She cuts at least 15 percent more than she will need.

ELAINE GOLAK

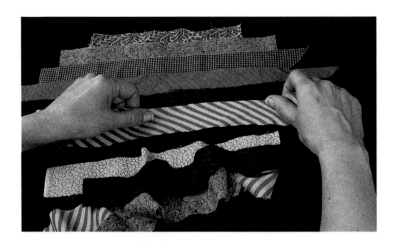

4

The quilt motif uses fabric strips to create the alternating diagonal square design. This pattern requires more than 50 cut strips. Elaine creates various diagonal patterns until the configuration reflects her idea.

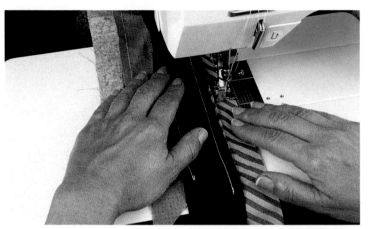

5

After the strips are cut and selected, she begins to machine sew them together. Using the Bernina 1630, she sews the pieces using a straight stitch. For more control on the foot pedal, Elaine removes her shoe.

6

The inside sashing separates the diagonal square patterns. It is cut in 2 inch widths from a brown on brown design. It is then sewn together with the four squares.

7

The material for the outer sash has a green on green floral print. This delicate design will serve to complement the composition without detracting from the other colors. The fabric is cut into 3 inch wide strips and sewn to the outer perimeter square to complete the top layer motif.

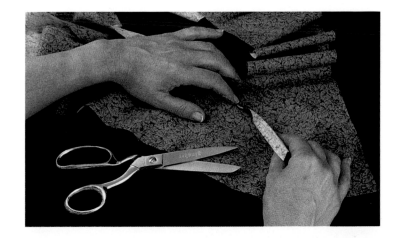

8

A paper template is cut in the shape of a hare. It is then pinned to the green outer border sash. The hare shape is cut out leaving a 1/8 inch border for stitching.

9

The green sash is machine sewn to the outer edge of the larger diagonal square pattern. The hares are ironed to the green sash using fusible interfacing, which secures their position during sewing.

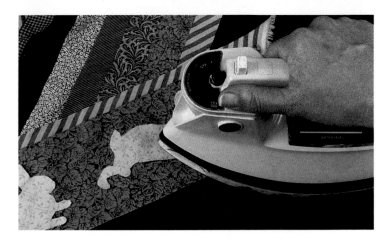

ELAINE GOLAK

10

Using the Bernina 1630 she machine sews a zigzag stitch with the number 1 presser foot. The horizontal and vertical width controls are used to create a tight satin stitch for the outline of the hare.

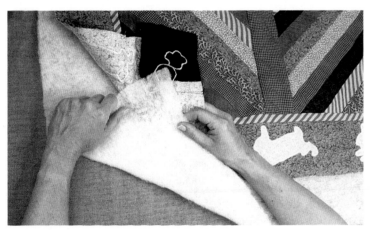

11

After the top layer is completed with the applique vegetables and running hares, it is ready to be quilted. The bottom layer of fabric is cut, together with a piece of polyester batting. The top layer is then placed in position and held down with safety pins.

12

A wooden hoop is attached to begin quilting. A basic quilting stitch is used to sew around the hare shapes and corner carrots. This equally spaced stitch will be used throughout the coverlet.

13

Once the diagonals are attached, the center circular design begins. A circle is cut from the same brown fabric used for the inside sashing. The edges are pressed under and pinned into place.

14

In keeping with the garden theme, Elaine appliques a cauliflower. This is created using a machine satin stitch in brown thread to define the shape. The edges of the circle are hand quilted through the layers.

15

A paper template is cut for the quilting pattern on the brown border. After it is pinned down, the shape is drawn with a white fabric pencil.

ELAINE GOLAK

16

The wooden hoop is attached to the area and secured. The circular pattern is quilted using a basic quilting stitch along the inner brown border.

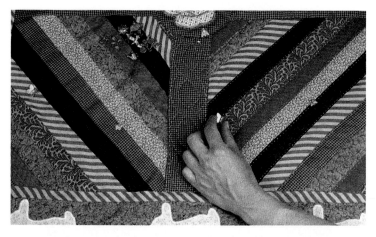

17

Several metal charms are positioned throughout the coverlet and delicately hand sewn. These complement the overall garden theme with the animal shapes.

18

After finishing the quilting and placing the charms, the binding is attached and sewn. The final element is the intricate hand stitching of a poem by Rudyard Kipling. *God gave all men all earth to love. But since our hearts are small, one spot should prove beloved overall.*

1

2

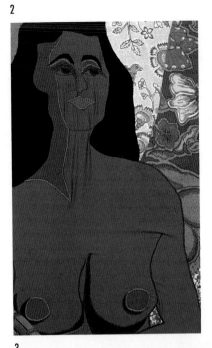

3

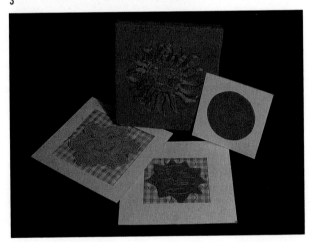

1
Nude *Private Collection*
Quilting
2
Island Lady *Private Collection*
Fabric Collage
3
Sun Series *Private Collection*
Threadwork

ELAINE GOLAK

4

4
Angel Series *Retail Display*
Soft Sculpture
5
Nude Series *Retail Display*
Soft Sculpture
6
Bristol Homes *Private Collection*
Soft Sculpture

5

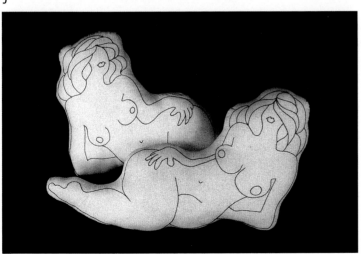

6

7

7
Theater Banner *The Acorn Theater Project*
Fabric Collage
8
Opening Season Banner *The Olney Theater*
Fabric Collage

8

ELAINE GOLAK

9

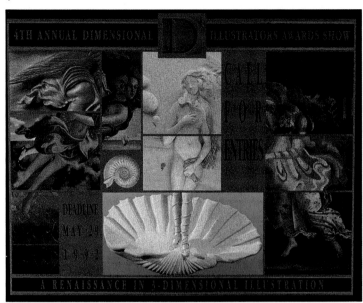

9
Call For Entries Poster *Dimensional Illustrators, Inc.*
Threadwork
10
Call for Entries Poster *Detail of Needlepoint*
Threadwork

10

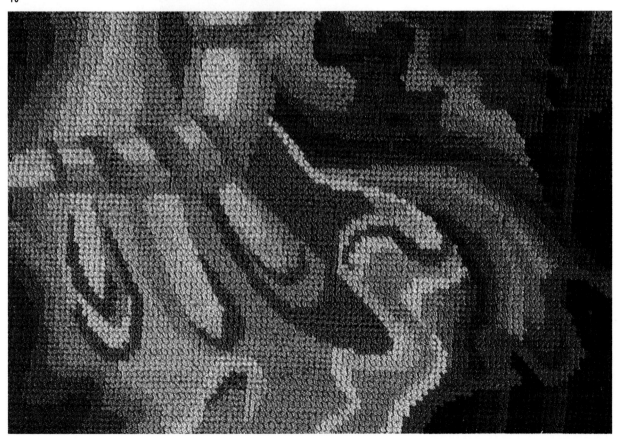

11

12

13

ELAINE GOLAK

14

15

16

15
Embroidered John Alcorn Illustration *Private Collection*
Threadwork
16
Embroidered Theorem *Private Collection*
Threadwork
17
Embroidered Bird *Private Collection*
Threadwork

17

ELAINE GOLAK

18

19

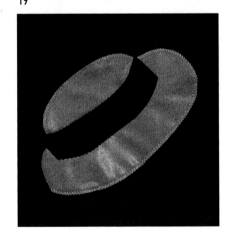

20

18
Madeline Banner *Strawbridge & Clothier*
Fabric Collage
19
Madeline's Hat *Strawbridge & Clothier*
Fabric Collage
20
Madeline's Dog *Strawbridge & Clothier*
Fabric Collage

21

22

21
Quilted Nude *Private Collection*
Quilting
22
Pamela *Private Collection*
Quilting
23
Heart Quilt *Private Collection*
Quilting

ELAINE GOLAK

23

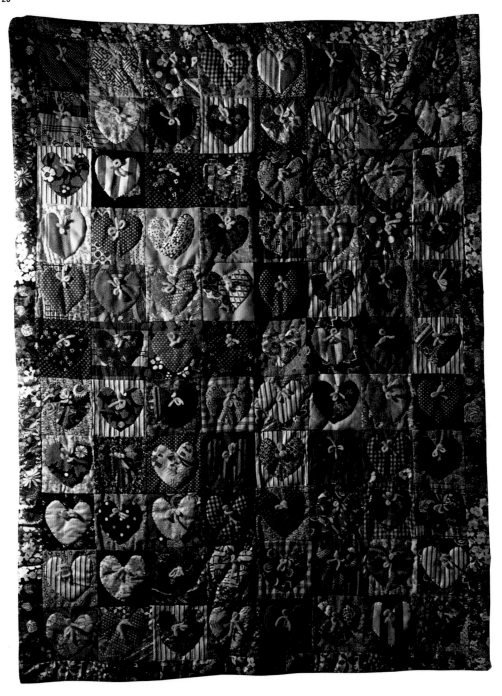

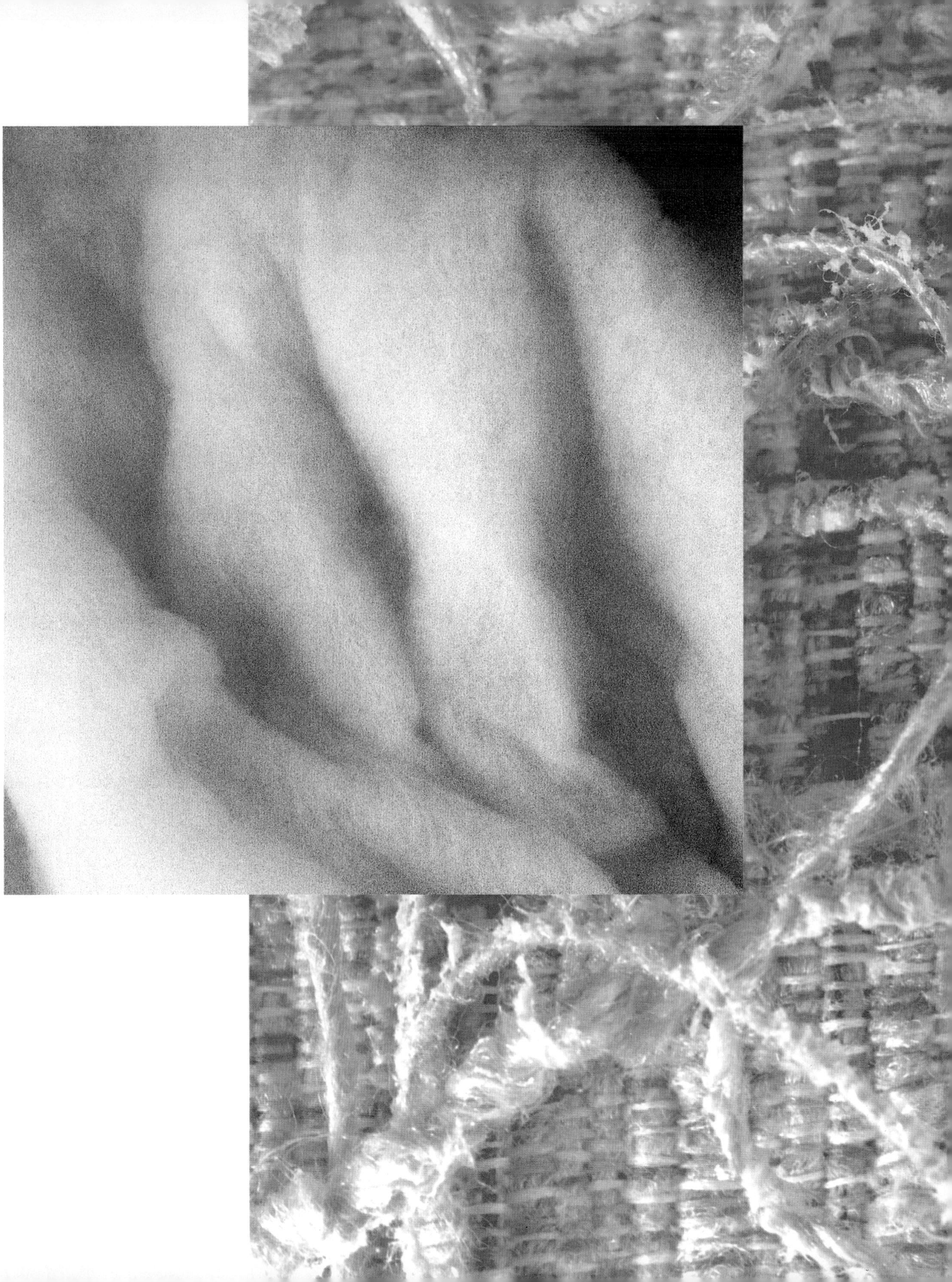

SOFT SCULPTURE

Soft sculpture has become a very popular form of fabric illustration. Fabric has the flexibility and resiliency to stretch around inner batting, foam or other materials with relative ease. These qualities combined with variations of texture and tone create highly diversified 3-Dimensional sculptures. Nancy Fouts and Lisa Lichtenfels are a marked contrast to the traditional soft sculpture artist. Their technical excellence and ingenious application enable them to use fabric in a very unconventional manner.

Although each artist's sculptural approach to the human elements of life is personal and intriguing, their methods and applications are strikingly different. Fouts' style is characterized by her use of icons and metaphorical symbols, which successfully capture the curiosity of the viewer. Lichtenfels manipulates facial expressions, emotions and gestures to convey an immediate sense of familiarity, warmth and novelty. The soft sculpture artistry of Fouts and Lichtenfels presents a uniquely creative approach to fabric illustration.

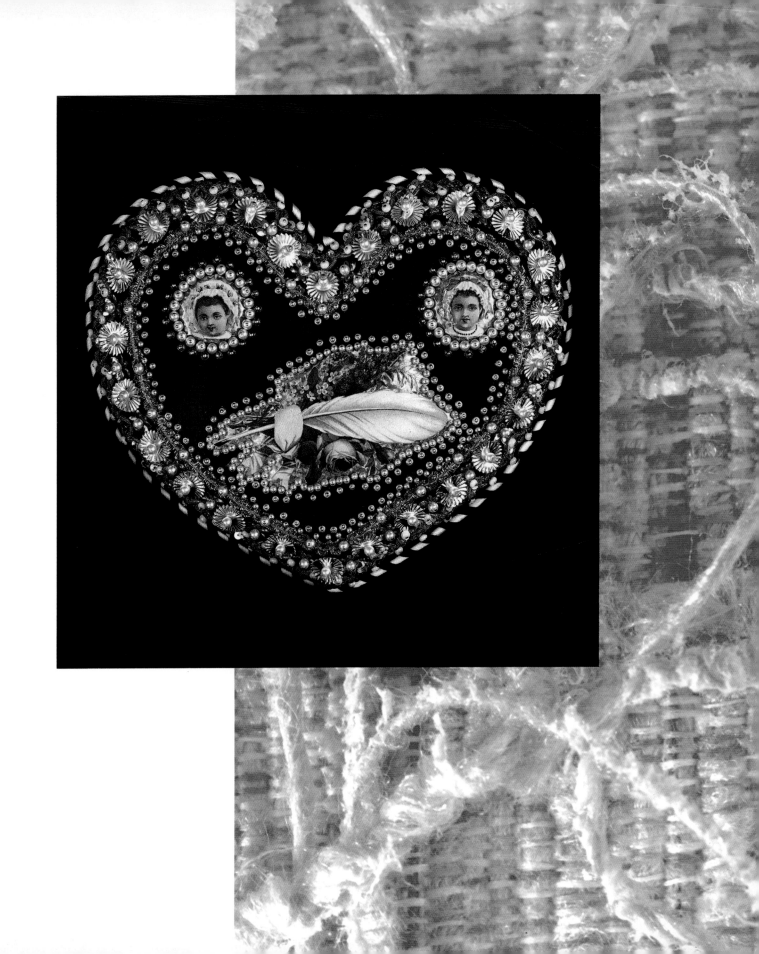

Nancy Fouts

Nancy Fouts has been in the business of creating dimensional models for more than 25 years. American born, Nancy came to England to study at the Chelsea School of Art. She has since earned a reputation for her singular fabric illustrations. Based in London, she and her husband, Malcolm Fowler, established Shirt Sleeve Studio to meet the vigorous demands of the British advertising industry. Fouts' notable images have made her a highly respected fabric artist. Her early professional work included illustrations for newspapers and magazines. Although skilled in many different media, Nancy feels most comfortable working in fabric. She prefers fabric sculpture because it affords her the artistic independence to experiment with a variety of textures.

Her creative philosophy is to let the original idea dictate the materials chosen. This is evident in her often surreal use of fabrics, which range from rare silk to everyday denim. She photographs work in progress to check camera angles and spot any problems. Fouts has created numerous Silk-Cut cigarette ads for Saatchi & Saatchi/London. She is highly regarded throughout the visual communication community for her imagery and extraordinary sense of design.

1

Antique ephemera is selected for use in the pearl sculpture heart. These printed pictures add a very personal element to the artwork. Pieces will be cut out and incorporated into the completed heart.

2

A variety of antique necklaces are selected. The pearls are removed and separated according to size. Each pearl opening must be large enough to pierce with a pin.

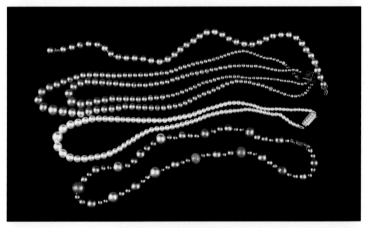

3

In addition to the ephemera and pearls, a variety of trims and glass beads are selected. Red velvet and numerous decorative tin shapes are chosen. The foil paper will become a background for the pictures.

NANCY FOUTS

4

Nancy decides to use a heart shape for the base.
A pattern is cut out of paper and used as a template.
The shape is then drawn on a piece of blue foam.

5

The heart shape is cut out using a scroll saw. The square
cut edges of the foam are filed to a smooth round radius
with a metal file.

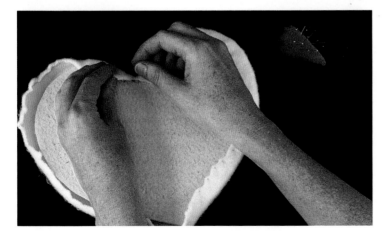

6

Batting is added to make a soft surface and pinned to
the back with dressmakers pins. As it is pinned, it is
slightly stretched to create a smooth, working surface
for the front.

7

Next, a piece of red velvet is cut larger than the foam heart. The velvet is then initially pinned in the front. The surface must be smooth and free of wrinkles.

8

The material is carefully folded over to the back. To keep the velvet smooth on the front surface, it is snipped every inch, pulled back and pinned.

9

Once the velvet is in place the trim is added. Black and white cotton piping is used for the perimeter border. This is attached with evenly spaced pins.

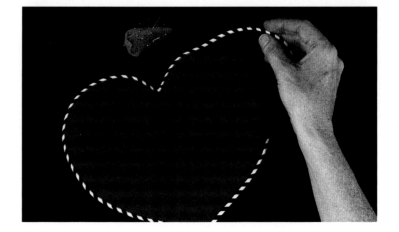

NANCY FOUTS

10

An inside border of gold sequin trim is attached. Glass beads are individually placed on each pin. They are then pierced through the sequin trim at equal intervals.

11

A pearl necklace is chosen for its small even pearls. They are attached by a pin to a gold tin floral shape then equally spaced around the inside of the sequin trim.

12

Silver tin shapes are placed on a pin shaft with a combination of pearl and pink beads at the top. These are then pinned in between the gold tin shapes.

13

Metallic gold braided trim is used to create an inner heart line. It is attached by pinning evenly spaced larger pearls around the edge.

14

Small ephemera figure heads and a floral feather print are chosen for the center. The white edges of the print are trimmed off with a scalpel blade.

15

Gold foil is cut larger than the ephemera shapes. This will be the decorative area where pins and pearls will be attached without piercing the actual print.

16

The figurehead and floral shapes are glued to the center of the foil pieces. They are secured in position by pins. A border of pins and large pearls are fastened side by side around the perimeter of the shapes.

17

Clear glass beads are attached to the pins. They are then pinned to the outer border and alternately spaced in between the pearls.

18

Metal and glass beads are used for the final border. They are alternately placed at intervals around the inside of the metallic gold braid trim. All the pins are then pushed down firmly and evenly into the foam.

1

2

3

1
Heart-No *Private Collection*
Soft Sculpture
2
Christmas Souvenir Anchor *Private Collection*
Soft Sculpture
3
Coupon Anchor *Private Collection*
Soft Sculpture

NANCY FOUTS

4

5

6

4
Valentine Heart *Private Collection*
Soft Sculpture
5
Maple Leaf Cushion *Air Canada*
Soft Sculpture
6
Heinz Tomato Ketchup *Heinz*
Threadwork

7

LOW TAR As defined by H.M. Government
Warning: SMOKING CAN CAUSE FATAL DISEASES
Health Departments' Chief Medical Officers

8

LOW TAR As defined by H.M. Government
Warning: SMOKING CAN CAUSE LUNG CANCER, BRONCHITIS AND OTHER CHEST DISEASES
Health Departments' Chief Medical Officers

NANCY FOUTS

9

501 LEVIS PORTATI AD OGNI ESPERIENZA.

7
Sculpture Man *Silk Cut Cigarettes*
Soft Sculpture
8
Chain Saw *Silk Cut Cigarettes*
Soft Sculpture
9
Man In Turban *Levi Jeans*
Soft Sculpture

120

10

11

Isn't it time NatWest helped you install central heating?

12

10
There's No Place Like Home
Newcastle Brown Ale
Threadwork
11
Igloo Sweet Igloo
National Westminster Bank
Threadwork
12
Floral Needlepoint *Interflora*
Threadwork

NANCY FOUTS

13

LOW TAR As defined by H.M. Government
STOPPING SMOKING REDUCES THE RISK OF SERIOUS DISEASES
Health Departments' Chief Medical Officers

14

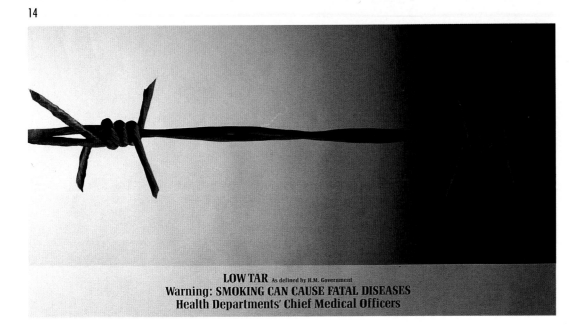

LOW TAR As defined by H.M. Government
Warning: SMOKING CAN CAUSE FATAL DISEASES
Health Departments' Chief Medical Officers

13
Scissor Ribbon *Silk Cut Cigarettes*
Soft Sculpture
14
Barbed Wire *Silk Cut Cigarettes*
Soft Sculpture

15

16

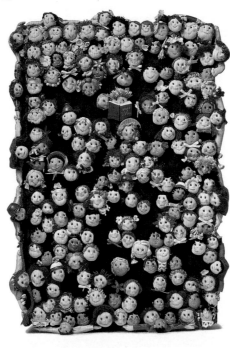

This summer, Club World seats come with pearl buttons
and Jermyn Street tailoring.

BRITISH AIRWAYS

15
Shirt Chair *British Airways*
Soft Sculpture
16
Book Jacket for Princess Diana *Capital Radio*
Soft Sculpture
17
Rose With Razors *Silk Cut Cigarettes Greece*
Soft Sculpture
18
Venus Fly Trap *Silk Cut Cigarettes*
Soft Sculpture
19
Face In Silk *Silk Cut Cigarettes*
Soft Sculpture

17

Το Υπουργείο Υγείας προειδοποιεί:
ΤΟ ΚΑΠΝΙΣΜΑ ΒΛΑΠΤΕΙ ΣΟΒΑΡΑ ΤΗΝ ΥΓΕΙΑ

NANCY FOUTS

18

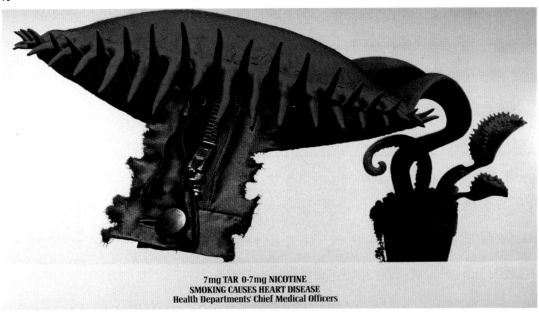

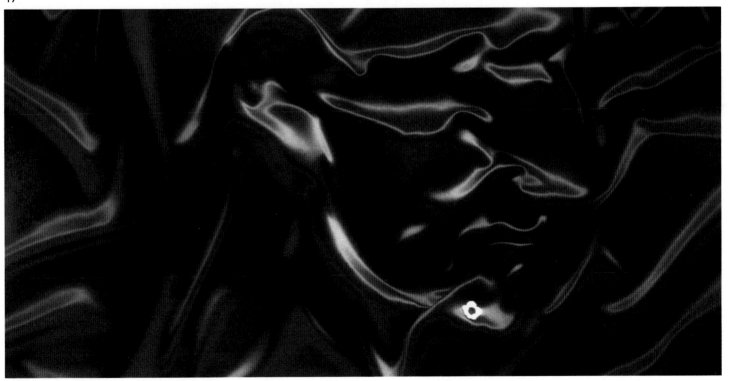

19

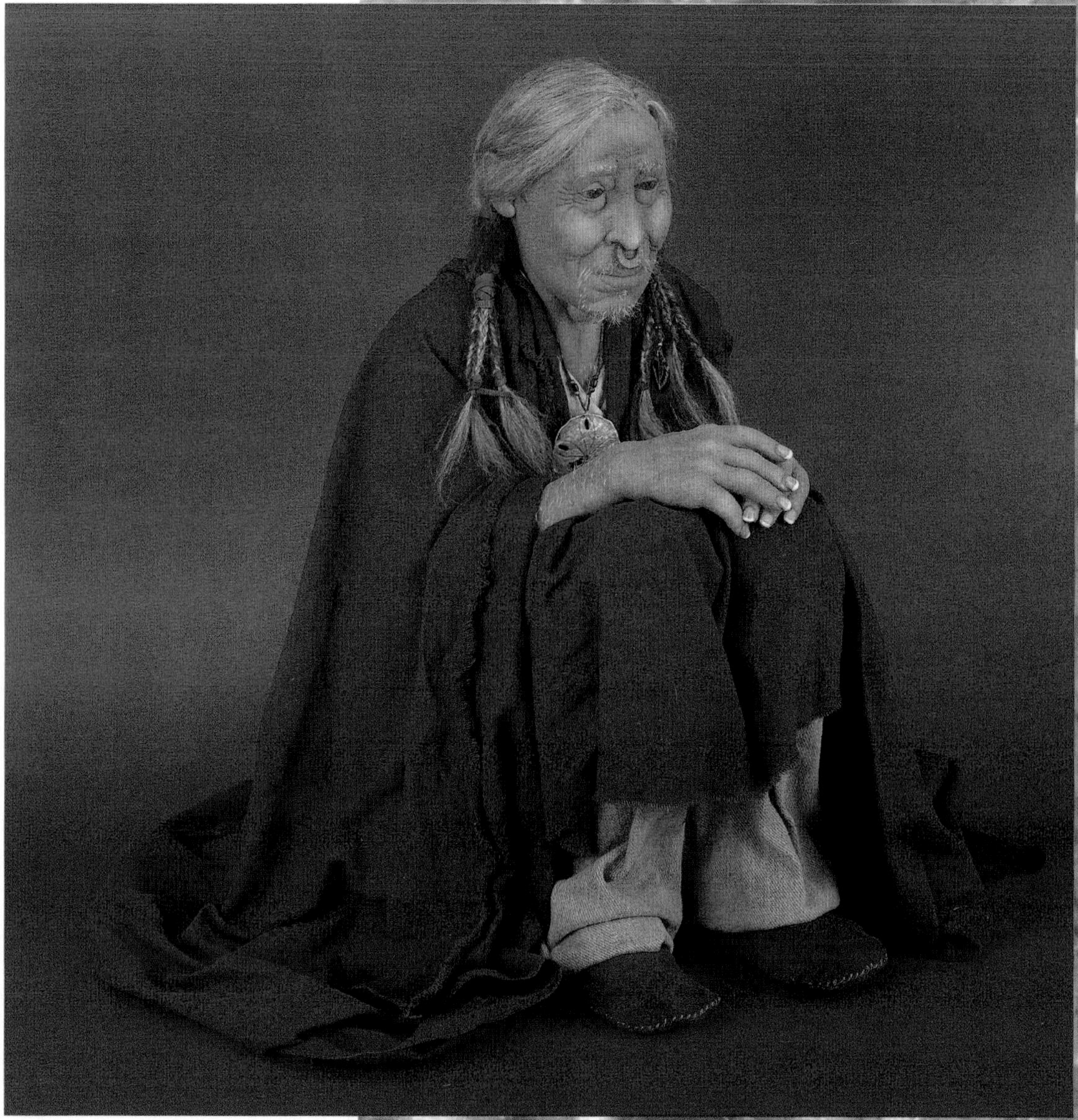

Lisa Lichtenfels

Lisa Lichtenfels takes fabric sculpture into an intriguingly realistic yet familiar dimension. Although fabric is not a medium associated with extreme realism, Lisa creates a unique world of life-like soft sculpture characters. Her artwork is exact and technical, yet exceptionally authentic. Lisa uses nylon stocking material to create her sculptures, because she feels it has the look and physical characteristics of flesh. She prefers working in fabric because it gives her the license to experiment and invent as she creates. Her work is tedious and requires detailed understructures, which support the sculptural elements of the model.

Lisa's prior experience includes work for Walt Disney Studio. She currently heads her own soft sculpture company. As a fabric illustrator she has created models for advertising agencies, animation studios and produced several private doll collections. Although she has worked as a fabric sculptor for fourteen years, Lisa views soft sculpture as a relatively new and challenging medium. "In many ways, fabric is a superior medium to the other "hard" mediums. It is warmer, richer and visually approachable. Fabric is a difficult medium for sculpting, unless you have a feel for the fabric." Lisa's unique models have earned her the esteem and admiration of creative visual artists worldwide.

1

Initial full size pencil sketches are drawn to establish the sitting pose and general gesture of the Indian man. He is an aboriginal American Indian from the Pacific Northwest and will be dressed in traditional clothing.

2

Tracing paper is placed over the drawings and the internal skeleton is planned. Using the front and side views as a guide, the armature for the body is constructed. The hand is initiated by tracing the hand diagram in copper wire.

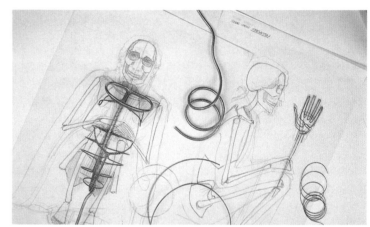

3

As the skeletal structure begins to take shape, the spine is formed from soft aluminum wire. Heavier steel wire reinforces the ribs and pelvis. The elements are connected by wrapping galvanized 24 gauge wire around the intersecting positions.

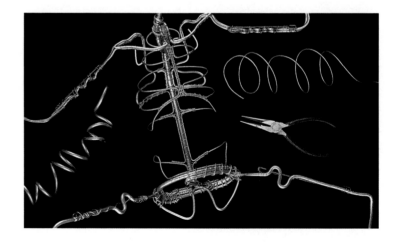

LISA LICHTENFELS

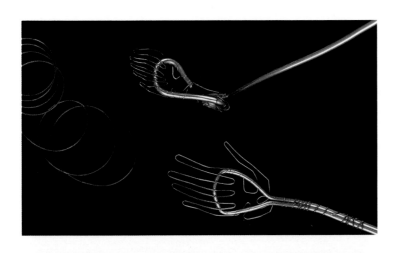

4

The hands and feet are created from 18" gauge copper wire. The bends in the palm are used to change the length of the fingers. This detailed understructure establishes the gesture of the hands.

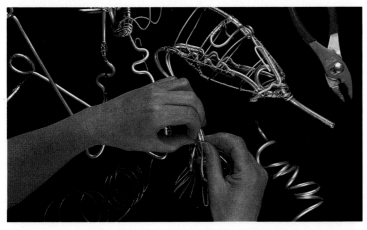

5

A 1/8 inch aluminum wire is used for the general structure of the arms and hands. The copper wire hand is attached by using the small steel wire to bond the two elements together.

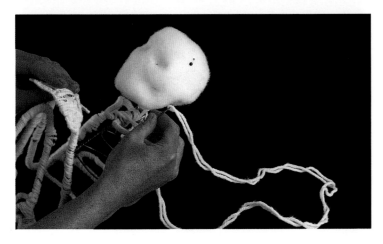

6

The entire skeleton is wrapped in baby yarn and regular yarn. This covers the harsh edges and creates a foundation for the next steps. The foam skull is covered in a layer of batting.

7

Wire inserts are formed to follow the contour shape of the eyebrows, eyes, nose and mouth. The inserts are pushed firmly into the foam skull so they will not move when wrapped in the nylon stocking.

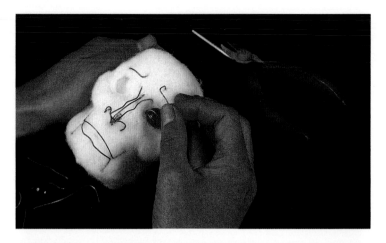

8

After forming the facial features in wire, they are covered in white nylon. The nylon is then pinned into position and firmly sewn into place to create a suitable base for the batting.

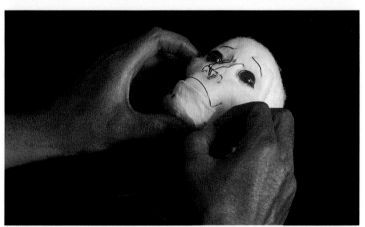

9

Batting is used to build up the muscles and flesh of the face. Layers are first pinned, then sewn into place until the contours of the features are exact. Marbles are delicately painted and shellacked to simulate real eyes.

LISA LICHTENFELS

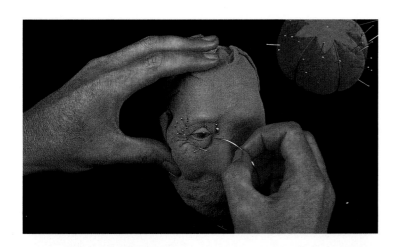

10

After the batting is finished, nylon is applied to the surface of the face. The wrinkles and remaining features are sewn into place with a circular needle and clear thread. The thread is hidden in the folds of the wrinkles. The understructure prevents the tension of the thread from flattening and distorting the face.

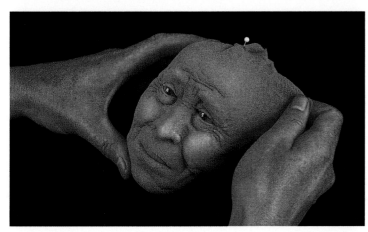

11

A second piece of nylon is sewn over the lip area and delicately needle-modeled. The excess nylon on the face is pulled back and pinned. The facial hair is applied last.

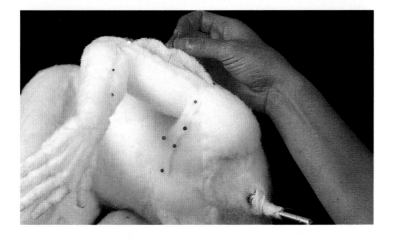

12

Using the same technique as the skull, the yarn wrapped skeleton is covered in layers of batting and fiberfill to simulate the muscle structure. Pieces of batting are pinned into place.

13

Many layers of fiberfill are stuffed between the batting and the covered surface is sewn into place. The exact muscle definition is important in achieving accurate anatomy.

14

The forearms are covered in nylon stocking and pinned into place. Later, the entire surface will be sewn into position. Once the nylon is in place, the sculpture must be handled carefully to avoid running.

15

The hands and fingers are needle-modeled with clear thread. Dyed green yarn is strategically placed on the hands to simulate the veins. It is now pinched and intricately needle-modeled.

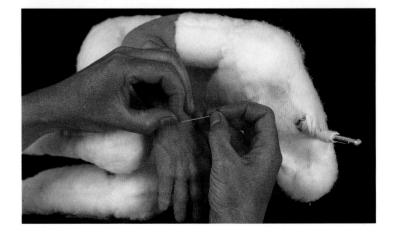

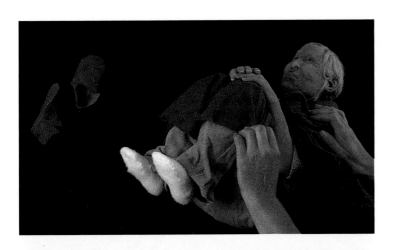

16

The head and body with the finished skin are attached. The head is covered with wig hair and the clothing is sewn onto the body. Handmade moccasins are placed on the feet.

17

The hair is braided, tied with leather strips and decorated with feathers and fur. Facial and arm hair is sewn in piece by piece. The nails are created from plastic then painted. The realistic tribal dress is reproduced from late 19th century photographs.

18

The sculpture is positioned to achieve gesture and character. The outer clothing is draped into position. Final adjustments are made to the folded hands.

1

2

1
Madonna and Child *Private Collection*
Soft Sculpture
2
Somali Man *Private Collection*
Soft Sculpture

LISA LICHTENFELS

3

4

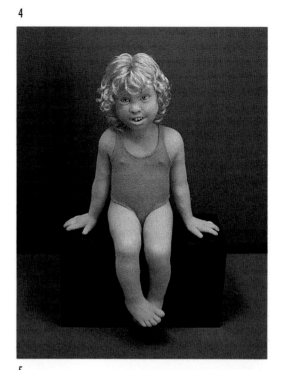

5

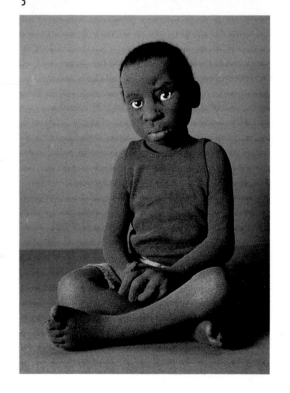

3
Bernadette *Private Collection*
Soft Sculpture
4
Nerissa *Private Collection*
Soft Sculpture
5
Raymond *Private Collection*
Soft Sculpture

134

6

7

8

6
Ticket Taker *Theater Design Circa 1930*
Soft Sculpture
7
Bette Midler *Private Collection*
Soft Sculpture
8
A Woman and Her Dog *Private Collection*
Soft Sculpture

LISA LICHTENFELS

9

10

9
Shawn *Private Collection*
Soft Sculpture
10
Shaman *Private Collection*
Soft Sculpture
11
Woman With a Question *Private Collection*
Soft Sculpture

11

12

13
The Smoker *Private Collection*
Soft Sculpture
14
Bob's Pan *Private Collection*
Soft Sculpture

13

LISA LICHTENFELS

14

15

16

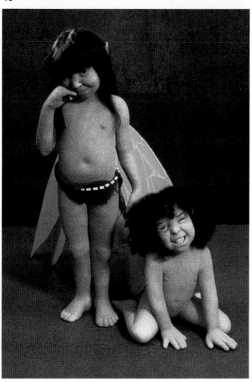

14
Willa *Private Collection*
Soft Sculpture
15
Anne *Private Collection*
Soft Sculpture
16
Fairies *Private Collection*
Soft Sculpture

17

18

19

17
Woman as Egg *Private Collection*
Soft Sculpture
18
Demi *Private Collection of Demi Moore*
Soft Sculpture
19
Delores *Private Collection*
Soft Sculpture

LISA LICHTENFELS

20

21

20
Fairie Queen *Private Collection*
Soft Sculpture
21
Allison *Private Collection*
Soft Sculpture

22

23

24

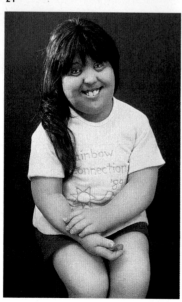

22
Phebe From the Opera *Conversation Piece*
Soft Sculpture
23
Grandmother *Theater Design Associates*
Soft Sculpture
24
Beloved *Private Collection*
Soft Sculpture

LISA LICHTENFELS

25

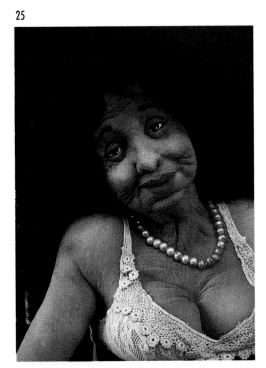

26

25
Riviera Mermaid *Private Collection*
Soft Sculpture
26
Broken Fairie *Private Collection*
Soft Sculpture
27
Petticoats and Parasols Doll Club
Convention Display
Soft Sculpture

27

142

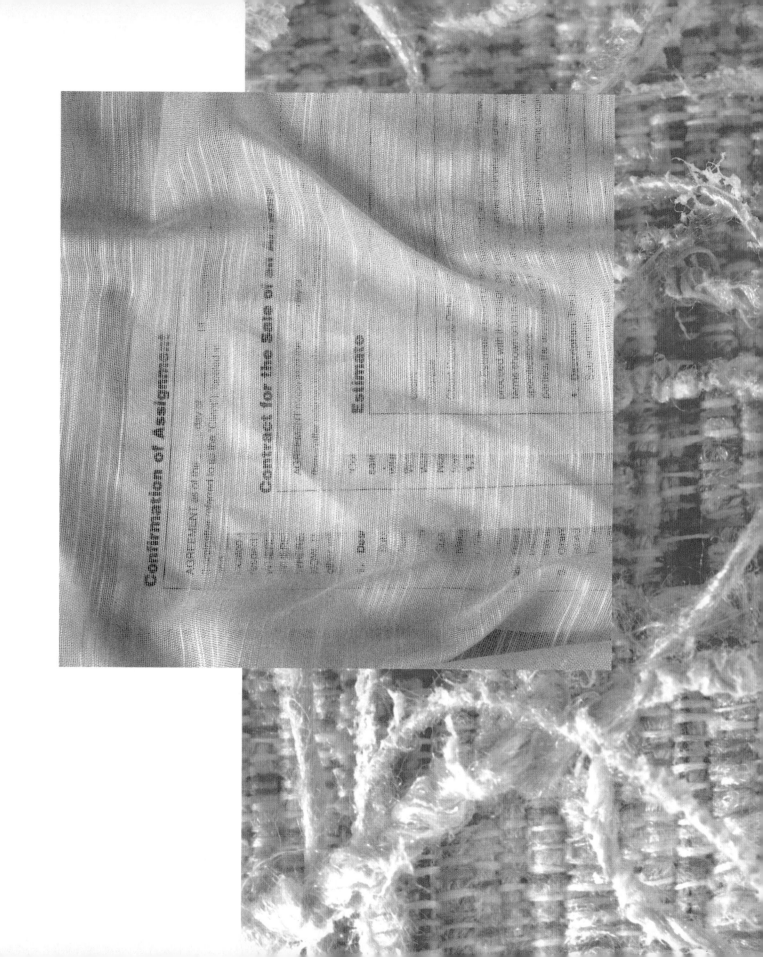

ARTIST'S RIGHTS

Fabric sculpture is currently enjoying a renaissance in the visual communication market. Today's fabric illustrators demonstrate the numerous applications of fabric as a viable medium for illustration. The talented fabric artists featured in this guidebook all share a variety of challenges regarding the sale and reuse of their art work. Ordinarily, the client buys a photograph of the work or commissions the sculpture as an original work of art. Each aspect of the sale can be financially beneficial for both parties. Understanding your rights as an artist is a salient ingredient for the successful marketing of the work.

Compensation will vary according to usage and rights sold. For fabric illustrations used in print advertising, fees are determined by use of the artwork as well as the reputation of the artist, the value derived by both parties and other factors. The artist customarily sells one time reproduction rights to the transparency of the work, according to a negotiated fee. The artist has the right to be compensated every time the transparency is reused.

Exclusive or unlimited rights agreements may exceed the client's need, but if needed will generally be compensated accordingly, in consideration of the myriad uses for the artwork. The artist reserves the right to be compensated every time the work is reproduced. In the case of gallery work, the artist may sell the sculpture for the purpose of display only. Under this agreement, the buyer only retains the right to display the model and may not photograph the work. All remaining copyrights are held by the creator of the work.

The contract between the artist and the client must specify, in writing, all rights being transferred to the client. These rights and the value of such rights should be included in the written contract. Any changes or additions to the work, initiated by the client, are billed separately to the client. All rights not transferred in the agreement remain the exclusive rights of the artist.

In addition, an agreement between the creator of the work and the photographer should be signed. Depending upon specific circumstances, the photographer and the artist may choose to share the rights to the photograph, which is considered a derivative of the work. This contract should outline the shared rights of ownership and compensation, if any, between the parties. The usage and fee is preferably agreed upon, in writing, before the sale to the client. All contracts should specify the exact usage being transferred to the client. It is strongly advised that all rights being transferred be described separately. It is generally understood that the greater the usage or number of rights that are sold the greater the compensation. The artist must state the specific usage and rights being transferred to the buyer and their fair market value.

A contract can offer an artist specific protection under the law and should be obtained whenever possible. Freelance artists should avoid signing work-for-hire contracts. Under the work-for-hire provisions of the copyright law, the illustrator forfeits copyright, authorship, credit and recognition rights for the work. A work-for-hire contract often prohibits the artist from reproducing, distributing or displaying the work in his or her portfolio. Also, the work can be reused, altered or mutilated by the owner without compensation to the artist.

The U.S. Constitution established copyright laws to protect the rights of the artist. Any infringement of these rights may be subject to severe penalties under these laws. For further information regarding protection of artist's rights, contact the Graphic Artists Guild. The Guild produces a handbook entitled ***Graphic Artists Guild Handbook: Pricing & Ethical Guidelines***, an important industry resource on rights and pricing. This must-have-reference guide discusses ethical standards, professional issues, practices and pricing. Standard contract forms are included for all artists. The Graphic Artists Guild was established in 1967 by professional artists concerned with industry guidelines, professional practices, ethical treatment of artists and fair market value for commissioned artwork. This organization is dedicated to assuring ethical standards between all artists and art buyers.

Fabric illustrators face difficult challenges creating, photographing and marketing their work. The techniques outlined in each chapter will guide you in understanding the numerous applications of fabric as an illustrative medium. ***Fabric Sculpture: The Step-By-Step Guide and Showcase*** is designed to help you understand the techniques of fabric sculpture presented by the foremost professionals in the industry.

Artist's Directory

ANNE COOK
96 Rollingwood Drive
San Rafael, CA 94901
415.454.5799 Telephone
415.454.0834 Fax

Clients Include:
Avon Books
Beatrice Foods
Becton-Dickson
C.R. Gibson
Holiday Inn
Levi's
Marriott Corporation
Medical Economics Magazine
Metropolitan Life
Modern Maturity Magazine
Nabisco
Ortho
Penguin USA
Putnam Berkley Press
Reader's Digest
Roman Meal
Weight Watchers
Woman's Day Magazine
Yankee Publishing

Awards
Bronze Awards, Dimensional Illustration Awards Show
Merit Awards, Dimensional Illustration Awards Show

MARGARET CUSACK
124 Hoyt Street
Brooklyn, NY 11217-2215
718.237.0145 Telephone
718.237.2430 Fax

Clients Include:
American Express
Aunt Millie's
Avon
Bloomingdale's
Dell
Howard Johnson
Little, Brown & Company
Macmillan
Maxwell House Coffee
Sony Music
The New York Times
Peek Freans
RCA
Reader's Digest
Seagram's
Singer
Texaco

Awards
Gold Award, Dimensional Illustration Awards Show
Silver Awards, Dimensional Illustration Awards Show
Bronze & Merit Awards, Dimensional Illustration Awards Show
Emmy Award, 1971
Pratt Institute Alumni Achievement Award, 1988
Print Magazine, 1985-88
Society of Illustrators 1974, 1981-85
Society of Publication Designers, 1975-6
The Art Annual, 1976, 1981
The One Show, 1975
Andy Award, 1975

NANCY FOUTS
Shirt Sleeve Studio
52 Oakley Square
London, England NW1 1NJ
071.388.6491 Telephone/Fax

Clients Include:
Abbott Mead Vickers
Benson & Hedges
Edinburgh Zoo
GGT
London Transport Tube
McCann Erickson/UK
Ogilvy & Mather/London
Saatchi & Saatchi/London
Sunday Express Magazine
WCRS/London
Young & Rubicam/London

Awards
Gold Awards, Dimensional Illustration Awards Show
Silver Awards, Dimensional Illustration Awards Show
Bronze & Merit Awards, Dimensional Illustration Awards Show
Gold Award, Design & Art Direction/London
Silver Award, Design & Art Direction/London

Elaine Golak
3000 Ford Road / #F11
Bristol, PA 10007
215.785.3368 Telephone

Clients Include:
Christine Taylor Home Designs
Duplex Display
J. E. Caldwell
Strawbridge & Clothier
Tiffany & Company

Awards
Bronze Award, Dimensional Illustration Awards Show
Merit Award, Dimensional Illustration Awards Show

ANN MORTON
1420 East Berridge Lane
Phoenix, AZ 85014
602.248.8055 Telephone
602.248.8055 Fax

Clients Include:
Big 4 Restaurants, Inc.
DelWebb Corporation
DMB Associates
Merrill-Lynch Hubbard, Inc.
Salt River Project
Time Warner
Vim & Vigor Magazine
Walt Disney Company
Westcor Partners

Awards
Silver Award, Dimensional Illustration Awards Show
Merit Award, Dimensional Illustration Awards Show
The Arizona Prisma Awards Show, 1984-93
Print Regional Annuals, 1985-91
Communication Arts, 1986,1989

LISA LICHTENFELS
Soft Sculpture Studio
146 Bay Street
Springfield, MA 01109
413.781.1359 Telephone

Clients Include:
Alan Epstien Photography
Giltspur
Graphics Unlimited
Kinetics Studio
McKinlay & Partners
Theatre Design Associates

Awards
Bronze Award, Dimensional Illustration Awards Show
Jumeau Award, Leading Female Artist 4th World Congress, 1994

JERRY PAVEY
9903 Markham Street
Silver Spring, MD 20901
800.618.3377 Telephone/Fax

Clients Include:
American Association of Retired Persons
Bell Atlantic
C & P Telephone
Dialogue Magazine
Earle Palmer Brown Advertising
Goodwill Industries of America
International Fabricare Institute
Macmillan Publishing
McGraw-Hill Publishing
Mobil Corporation
Pfizer Pharmaceuticals
S.D. Warren Paper Company
The Brookings Institute
UNICEF
US Information Agency
US Postal Service

Awards
Silver Awards, Dimensional Illustration Awards Show
Bronze & Merit Awards, Dimensional Illustration Awards Show
Gold & Silver ADDY Awards, Advertising Club of Washington
Gold Medal, Society of Illustrators
Gold Medals, New York ACE Awards Show
Gold Medal, New York Museum of American Illustration
Gold Medals, Art Directors Club of Washington
Gold Medal, New York Art Directors Club
Gold Medals & Special Gold Innovation Medals, Printing Industries of America

150

Dimensional Illustrators, Inc.

Kathleen Ziegler

Nick Greco

In 1985, Kathleen Ziegler and Nick Greco established Dimensional Illustrators, Inc. to create 3-Dimensional illustrations for the visual communications industry. Kathleen specializes in creating 3-D models for the pharmaceutical, advertising, publishing and television industries. Kathleen's design mediums include plastic, clay, acrylics, paper, wood and foam.

Her work has appeared in Discover, Health, Nursing, Learning, Veterinary Economics, Drug Therapy, Medical Economics and Obstetrics and Gynecology. Kathleen has been recognized for her design acumen by the Association of Medical Illustrators Show, the Desi Awards Show and the Philadelphia Art Directors Club Show. Clients include, Cigna Corporation, Smith Kline Beecham, Ciba-Geigy, Park Davis, Centrum and Harper & Row.

An accomplished lecturer, Kathleen has participated in numerous seminars on 3-Dimensional illustration including the Association of Medical Illustrators, The University of the Arts in Philadelphia, Graphix '90 in New York and the Royal College of Art in London, England. She has been featured in Step-By-Step Graphics and her signature style is recognized throughout the communications industry.

As a principal partner of Dimensional Illustrators, Inc., Nick Greco concentrates his efforts on marketing the 3-Dimensional designs of the company. Nick negotiates contracts, sets pricing guidelines and establishes usage and copyrights. He has lectured both in the United States and London on the copyright laws pertaining to the sale and usage rights of 3-Dimensional illustrations. As director of the 3-Dimensional Art Directors and Illustrators Awards Show, Nick coordinates the only international awards show honoring the best of the best in 3-Dimensional illustration.

Together Kathleen and Nick have focused their efforts towards advancing the recognition of 3-Dimensional illustration as a viable and notable adjunct of the communications industry. The 3-Dimensional Art Directors and Illustrators Awards Show is held annually at the Art Directors Club of New York. This prestigious show is dedicated to showcasing the best in 3-D advertising worldwide.

Call For Entries

CALL FOR ENTRIES

Calling all Art Directors, 3-Dimensional Illustrators, Modelmakers, Animators and Students to enter their work in the Annual Dimensional Art Directors & Illustrators Awards Show. This singular showcase of 3-Dimensional Illustration is dedicated to celebrating excellence in 3-D design in the advertising and publishing industry. All professionals, creatively associated with 3-D Illustration, are invited to submit their work in this singular design competition. Be recognized for your creative excellence in the only competition honoring 3-Dimensional Illustration worldwide.

ELIGIBILITY

All published or unpublished work may be submitted in the dimensional mediums and categories listed. Work must have been created during the past 3 years. DO NOT SUBMIT ORIGINAL WORK. Dimensional Illustrators, Inc. reserves the right to reassign an entry into a more appropriate category. Student entries must include photocopy of student ID. Decisions of the judges are final. All winners will be notified by September.

PREPARATION OF ENTRIES

Print Entries

Attach one Entry Label or facsimile to the back of each entry. Submit unmounted tearsheets, brochures, photographs, posters, transparencies or slides from the appropriate mediums and categories listed. Posters may be submitted on 35mm slides. (No Glass) (Entry materials will be returned if self-addressed pre-paid envelope is provided. DO NOT SEND ORIGINAL WORK).

3-D Animation Entries

Submit video entries on NTSC, American Standard 3/4" video tape only. DO NOT USE PAL. Attach an Entry Label to each cassette box. For international entries send English script and list all titles in English. Dimensional Illustrators, Inc. reserves the right to reassign an entry into a more appropriate category.

AWARDS

All accepted entries will receive Gold, Silver and/or Bronze awards for creative excellence. Gold and Silver award winning Art Directors and Dimensional Illustrators will be presented awards at the opening night reception.

ENTRY FEES

Single Entry: $25.
Campaign: $45. *(3-5 Related Pieces Maximum)**
Video: $50. Each
Video Campaign: $85. *(3-5 Related Videos Maximum)**
Student Single: $10.
Student Campaign: $20. *(3-5 Related Pieces Maximum)**
*All campaigns are judged as one entry.

One check or international money order in U.S. currency (drawn on a U.S. bank) payable to **Dimensional Illustrators, Inc.** must accompany all entries. Foreign checks not drawn on a US bank are ineligible. Entry fees are not refundable.

All entrants will be notified of acceptance or regrets. All winners will be exhibited, in their PRINTED form, at the Art Directors Club of New York. Every accepted entry will be reproduced with credits in the **3-Dimensional Illustrators Awards Annual.** Upon acceptance, a hanging fee will be required as follows: Single: $60. Campaign: $85. Video: $80. Video Campaign: $120. Student Single: $20. Student Campaign: $25.

EXHIBITIONS

New York Art Directors Club/USA

Gold, Silver and Bronze winners from the Annual Dimensional Illustrators Awards Show will be exhibited at the New York Art Directors Club, 250 Park Avenue South, New York, NY.

CATEGORIES

EDITORIAL: Consumer Magazine
1. Cover
2. Full Page
3. Less Than Full Page
4. Spread
5. Campaign *(3-5 pieces maximum)*

EDITORIAL: Business Trade Magazine
6. Cover
7. Full Page
8. Less Than Full Page
9. Spread
10. Campaign *(3-5 pieces maximum)*

NEWSPAPERS:
11. Editorial *(Full Page/Spread)*
12. Editorial Campaign *(3-5 pieces maximum)*
13. Advertising *(Full Page/Spread)*
14. Advertising Campaign *(3-5 pieces maximum)*
15. Sunday Supplement

BOOKS:
16. Cover or Jacket
17. Inside Page
18. Complete Book *(Campaign Fee)*
19. Series *(Campaign Fee)*

CHILDREN'S BOOKS:
20. Cover or Jacket
21. Inside Page
22. Complete Book *(Campaign Fee)*
23. Series *(Campaign Fee)*

ADVERTISING DIRECT MAIL: Consumer
24. Brochure Cover
25. Brochure *(Campaign Fee)*

ADVERTISING DIRECT MAIL: Business
26. Brochure Cover
27. Brochure *(Campaign Fee)*

ANNUAL REPORT:
28. Cover
29. Complete Annual Report *(Campaign Fee)*

ADVERTISING: Consumer Magazine
30. Full Page
31. Less Than Full Page
32. Spread
33. Campaign *(3-5 pieces maximum)*

ADVERTISING: Business Trade Magazine
34. Full Page
35. Less Than Full Page
36. Spread
37. Campaign *(3-5 pieces maximum)*

AUDIO/VIDEO: Cover
38. Record, CD, Tape, Video, Software

CALENDAR:
39. Full Page
40. Complete Calendar *(Campaign Fee)*

3D ILLUSTRATION:
Entries in this category are judged solely on the craftsmanship of the 3-Dimensional Illustration.

41. ADVERTISING
42. EDITORIAL

SELF PROMOTION:
43. Flyer, Postcard, Business Card

UNPUBLISHED:
44. (Send slide or print)

DIMENSIONAL TV ANIMATION:
45. TV Commercial
46. Music Video
47. Public Service
48. Self Promotion

GREETING CARDS:
49. Single
50. Campaign *(3-5 pieces maximum)*

POSTERS:
51. Advertising
52. Editorial
53. Self-Promotion
54. Public Service
55. Limited Edition
56. Poster Campaign *(3-5 pieces maximum)*

MISCELLANEOUS:
57. Any applied use of 3-Dimensional illustration in the print media not included above. Send tearsheet, photograph or 35mm slide. (No Glass)

ENTRY FORM:

Fill in One Entry Form and send One Check to cover all entries, payable to **Dimensional Illustrators, Inc.**

Entrant	
Contact Person	
Firm	
Address	
City	**State**
Country	**Postal Code/Zip**
Phone	**Fax**

Number of Entries:

____	Singles	x $25.	=	$ _____
____	Campaigns	x $45.	=	$ _____
____	Videos	x $50.	=	$ _____
____	Video Campaigns	x $85.	=	$ _____
____	Student Singles	x $10.	=	$ _____
____	Student Campaigns	x $20.	=	$ _____
____	TOTAL ENTRIES			$ _____
				TOTAL ENCLOSED

Signature of Entrant   Date

Method of Payment:

Payable to **Dimensional Illustrators, Inc.**

___ Check   ___ Money Order
___ International Money Order
___ Master Card   ___ Visa

Card Number

Expiration Date

Signature   Date

SEND TO:

Annual 3-D Awards Show
362 Second Street Pike / Suite 112
Southampton, PA 18966 USA
PHONE 215.953.1415 **FAX** 215.953.1697

DEADLINE: ANNUALLY MAY 31

MAIL-IN CHECKLIST

1. Attach ENTRY LABEL or facsimile to the back of EACH unmounted tearsheet, photo, transparency, slide or 3/4" videotape.
2. Complete ONE ENTRY FORM and include ONE CHECK to cover all entries.
3. Make check payable to: **Dimensional Illustrators, Inc.**
4. Questions? Call (215) 953-1415 Fax (215) 953-1697
5. Mail entry materials to:
      Annual 3-D Awards Show
      362 Second Street Pike / Suite 112
      Southampton, PA 18966 USA

DEADLINE: ANNUALLY MAY 31

Attach this entry label or facsimile to the back of EACH entry. If entry is accepted, credits will be typeset for the Exhibition and Awards Annual. This will be the ONLY opportunity to provide credit information. Please check accuracy.

TYPE or PRINT clearly

CATEGORY NUMBER: _____

Mediums (Circle One)

A. Paper Sculpture	G. Clay Sculpture
B. Paper Collage	H. Mixed Media
C. Paper Pop-Up	I. Recycled Materials
D. Plastic Sculpture	J. Metal Sculpture
E. Fabric/Stitchery	K. Video 3-D Animation
F. Wood Sculpture	

ENTRANT

Contact Person

Art Director

3-D Illustrator

Paper Engineer

Agency

Studio

Photographer

Producer/Director

3-D Animator

Publisher

Client

School

Title of Entry (IMPORTANT)

Glossary

3-DIMENSIONAL ILLUSTRATION
The creation of a 3-Dimensional model that is photographed and used in print.

APPLIQUÉ
From the Latin applicare or French appliquer, the term refers to a decorative work where pieces of fabric are stitched or joined onto another larger fabric. Fabric collage creates a delicate, 3-Dimensional effect.

ARMATURE
A skeletal framework of metal or wood built as a support on which a fabric, clay or plaster model is constructed. Armatures are typically used in soft sculpture for added support.

BASIC QUILTING STITCH
It is fundamentally a running stitch in which the needle is always worked into the quilt from the top layer down.

BATTING
A cotton or polyester filler primarily used between the top and bottom layers of a quilt. In soft sculpture it is used to stuff the inside of the sculpture.

CARBON TRANSFER
A thin paper coated with carbon on one side. Images are transferred by placing a piece of fabric under the paper and pressing with a stylus or pencil.

CROSS STITCH

A stitching technique that crosses one thread over another. The two diagonal stitches cross at the center to form an X of various length.

CURVED NEEDLE

A needle used for heavy duty sewing where a straight needle would be cumbersome. Generally used for quilting or soft sculpture.

DRESSMAKER PINS

A pin designed for light or medium weight fabrics. The standard dressmaker pin or seamstress pin is 1-1/6 inch in length.

EMBROIDERY

Creating a pattern by working a needle with colored threads into a flat foundation. Many stitches can be used singly or in combination to create colorful design patterns.

FRENCH KNOT

An embroidery stitch in which thread is wrapped around the needle to form a knot on the fabric surface.

FUSIBLE INTERFACING

A synthetic heat sensitive strip of adhesive which is placed between two fabric layers and ironed to activate the adhesive. It is also applied to the back of a fabric to give it strength and support.

LEATHER THIMBLE

A piece of leather fitted with a metal insert that fits over the finger. Primarily used by quilters to provide greater flexibility.

MEXICAN BARK PAPER

Bark that is soaked in water with pulp, processed and pressed into thin paper sheets.

MOTIF

A small complete design which is repeated at intervals on the fabric.

MUSLIN

A plain woven fine to coarse cotton fabric. Used for backing on quilts or to cut patterns.

NEEDLEPOINT

A technique for making stitches on an open weave canvas. The canvas serves as the foundation for the stitchwork. The canvas is constructed of various gauges depending on the number of meshes per inch.

NEEDLEWORK

A general term used to describe any plain or decorative work created with a needle and thread including threadwork, appliqué or quilting.

PIPING

A decorative cord with a projecting flat strip of fabric which is stitched in a seam or along an edge.

PRESSER FOOT

A sewing machine accessory with special groves and guides to suit a particular sewing task. The presser foot controls the feed-through of the fabric.

QUILTING

The use of a running stitch to secure a soft filler between two layers of fabric. The top layer is the decorative side, the bottom layer is generally muslin and the filler can be cotton, flannel or polyester fiber batting. Quilting is primarily used for bedcovers, pillows, wall hangings or clothing.

QUILTING HOOP

A large hoop designed to hold all three layers of a quilt securely in position. They come in a variety of diameters and are designed to prevent shifting during sewing.

RUNNING STITCH

A small stitch used mainly for hand-stitched gathering. It is created by passing the needle in and out of the fabric forming a stitch of equal length.

THREADWORK

The creation of a design or pattern using thread as the overall medium. Includes embroidery, cross stitch, counted stitch and needlepoint.

ZIGZAG STITCH

A machine made lockstitch of specific side to side width and length. Widely used for edge-finishing or decorative work. A basic stitch used in appliqué work.

Production Credits

DEBORAH DAVIS is a graphic designer and typographer who lives and works in the Los Angeles area. Her design experience ranges from book and cover design to print production. Deborah has worked as a freelance graphic designer in all phases of book publishing. She enjoys designing books, book covers, posters and various materials for the publishing industry. Part of her time is spent donating her design expertise to various non-profit organizations.

JENNIFER DUNN is a freelance designer who lives in Philadelphia with her husband and two prized cats. She holds a Masters Degree in Visual Design from Southeastern Massachusetts University. Jennifer concentrates her graphic efforts on book designs and has worked as a consultant with many of the area's leading publishers. In addition, she applies her talents to the creation of brochures, promotional materials and posters. Her style, awareness and attention to detail contribute to her overall design sensitivity.

TOM MCCLINTOCK has worked as a freelance journalist since 1972. Presently, he works in the Philadelphia area and holds a Bachelor of Arts Degree in English Literature and Creative Writing. Tom specializes in personal interviews, music and entertainment columns and general feature writing. He currently applies his writing talents to articles on fiction, travel and leisure. As a freelance writer, he enjoys the freedom to explore a wide range of topics relating to the arts and entertainment industry.

Brumstead, Elaine. The Home Sewing Library Soft Furnishings. Ballantine Books, A Division of Random House, Inc., New York. and simultaneously in Canada by Random House of Canada Limited, Toronto. First American Edition: August, 1987

Caulfield, Sophia and Saward, Blanche. The Dictionary of Needlepoint. Blaketon Hall Ltd. England 1989

Gostelow, Mary. Consultant Editor. The Complete Guide to Needlework: Techniques and Materials. Chartwell Books, Inc., N.J., Quill Publishing Ltd., London.

The Reader's Digest Association, Inc. Complete Guide To Needlework. Second Printing, November, 1979

The Reader's Digest Association, Inc. Complete Guide To Sewing. Pleasantville, New York, Montreal, Canada 1976

This book was set in Caslon 3, Futura Book and Futura Condensed manufactured by Adobe. It was produced on the Macintosh using QuarkXPress.

Sewing machine supplied by Bernina.

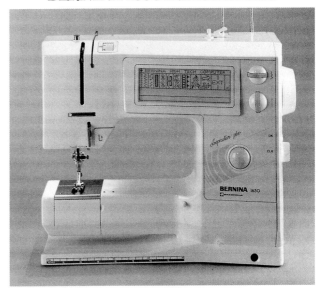